ADVANCE PRAISE FOR

But Darling, I'm Your Auntie Mame!

"Richard Tyler Jordan has written a revealing and entertaining history of Auntie Mame."

— ANGELA LANSBURY

"But Darling, Richard Tyler Jordan has caught all the fun and beautiful madness of *Auntie Mame* and the musical *Mame* worldwide. His book is a banquet."

— JEROME LAWRENCE, playwright
with Robert E. Lee of *Auntie Mame* & *Mame*

"Reading *But, Darling, I'm Your Auntie Mame!* brought back delightful memories of some of the most fulfilling theatrical experiences of my life. Richard Tyler Jordan has crafted a marvelous history of Mame Dennis and reminds us that Auntie Mame remains one of the most unforgettable – and cherished – heroines of 20th century literature, theatre and film."

— JO ANNE WORLEY, star,
multiple productions of *Mame*

"Mame Dennis will forever maintain a precious place in my heart. I've played her in both the play and the musical! The character has enriched my life, as I know it has enriched the lives of audiences the world over. Richard Tyler Jordan's *But Darling, I'm Your Auntie Mame!* is unlike any other book about show business I can recall. It is a brilliant tribute to one of the 20th century's greatest icons of fiction."

— CAROLE COOK, *Mame* & *Auntie Mame*

"Richard Tyler Jordan's adventure with Auntie Mame is great fun. Once I started devouring it, I couldn't stop."
– ROBERT OSBORNE, host,
Turner Classic Movies and
columnist, *The Hollywood Reporter*

"But Darling, I'm Your Auntie Mame! is a cover-to-cover delight. Not only a comprehensive history of a beloved character, but an insightful, often surprising, always entertaining story of the towering talents that have made Mame – in her many incarnations – this century's favorite daffy aunt.

"Jordan's obvious love of his subject matter rewards readers interested in serious research, behind-the-scenes trivia, eyewitness reports, celebrity anecdote, and lucid commentary. The result is a one-of-a-kind portrait of a one-of-a-kind woman, the dozens of talented women who have played her, and the hundreds of creative people to be found in the heart of our beloved Auntie Mame."
– JEFF KURTTI, author,
The Great Movie Musical Trivia Book
and *What Were They Thinking?*
The "Bad" Movie Musicals and How They Got That Way

"Richard Tyler Jordan's *But Darling, I'm Your Auntie Mame!* is just like Mame herself – outrageous, clever, witty, full of great good humor and rich insight. Richard Jordan has packed his book with solid research and great gossip. He also generously serves up the backstage truth about the parade of incomparable – and sometimes impossible – legendary showbiz ladies who played Mame over the years. More than Mame, this book is an irresistible ride through the golden ages of Broadway and Hollywood."
– COYNE STEVEN SANDERS, author, *Rainbow's End*

BUT DARLING, I'M YOUR AUNTIE MAME!

The Amazing History of the World's Favorite Madcap Aunt

But Darling, I'm Your Auntie Mame!

The Amazing History of the World's Favorite Madcap Aunt

Richard Tyler Jordan

CAPRA PRESS
SANTA BARBARA

For Billy Barnes

Cover jacket and book design by Frank Goad, Santa Barbara

LIBRARY OF CONGRESS CATALOGUING-IN-PULICATION DATA

Jordan, Richard Tyler, 1960-
But Darling, I'm your Auntie Mame! : the amazing history of the world's
favorite madcap aunt / Richard Tyler Jordan.
p.   cm.
ISBN 0-88496-430-2 (hardcover : alk. paper),
ISBN 0-88496-431-0 (paper : alk. paper)
1. Dennis, Patrick, 1921-1976 – Characters – Auntie Mame. 2. Theater –
United States – History – 20th century. 3. Dennis, Patrick, 1921-1976. Auntie
Mame. 4. Dennis Patrick, 1921-1976 – Adaptations. 5. Lawrence, Jerome,
1915- . Auntie Mame. 6. Mame, Auntie (Fictitious character) 7. Herman,
Jerry, 1933- . 8. Auntie Mame (Motion Picture) I. Title.
PS3554.E537Z7 1998
812'.54f--dc21   97-45826 CIP

Capra Press
Post Office Box 2068
Santa Barbara, CA 93120

Table of Contents

Acknowledgements

THE AUTHOR wishes to express his deepest and most heart-felt gratitude to numerous individuals who, over the course of researching and writing this book, have imparted memories and supported this project to fruition. This endeavor has been a labor-of-love from its inception. The value of the contributions made by the following individuals is inestimable. I am most indebted to:

Auntie Mame collaborators Jerome Lawrence and Robert E. Lee; the writers of the play *Auntie Mame* and the book of the musical *Mame* have my eternal gratitude for their ceaseless support and encouragement. Also, deep appreciation to Jerry Herman, whose words and music have enriched my life and the world. Furthermore, I thank him for graciously contributing the introduction to this book.

Sincere gratitude to Patrick Dennis' widow Louise Tanner, and son Michael Tanner, for providing private and personal correspondence from the late/great creator of Auntie Mame; and also to Lance Brisson, who magnanimously provided access to rare documents from the estate of his parents, Rosalind Russell and Frederick Brisson.

I am grateful to the following individuals for their clear and invaluable memories of their direct or indirect involvement with the Auntie Mame legacy: Cris Alexander, Charles Adams Baker, Joanna Barnes, Dorothy Blackburn, Henry Brandon, John Bowab, Coral Browne, Peggy Cass, Betty Comden, Jane Connell, Sumner Locke Elliott, Morton DaCosta, Clifford Fearl, Charles Forsythe, John Fricke, Robert Fryer, Beulah Garrick, Adolph Green, Margaret Hall, Jan Handzlik, Joseph Harris, Charlotte Jones, Mrs. Robert E.

Lee, Lucy Lee, Margaret Lewis, Ann Miller, James Monks, Jullian Muller, Stan Page, Phyillis Rab, John Reque, Polly Rowles, Coyne Steven Sanders, Gus Schirmer, Robert Smith, Allan Taylor, Vic Vallejo, Thomas J. Watson, Maury Weintrobe, Onna White, Ron Young and Paul Zindel. A special (and eternal) thank you to Muriel Pollia, Ph.D. – for "opening doors I never dreamed existed."

To my parents, Patricia E. & Benjamin P. Jordan. Also, Albe Albelo, Bart Andrews, Frank Andrews, Teri Avanian, Tom Avilla, Clark Bason, Robin Blakely & Mark Stroginis, Cheryl Brooks, Judy & Don Bustany, Gary Carver. Patricia Collins, Carole Cook and Tom Troupe, Cathy Doub, Elaine Espindle, Helen Frost, Mike Funicello, David Galligan, Paul Gilger, Howard Green, Denise Greenawalt, Anthony, Louise, David & Rita Grappi, Tami Hanson, Jane A. Johnston & George D. Wallace, Dana Jordan & Bob Lowe, Robert & Jacqueline Jordan, James Jordan, Jackie Joseph, Pat Kavanagh, Jane Klain, Alan Kramer, Jeff Kurtti, Angela Lansbury, Al Morley, Karen Morrow, Barry Moss, Mary Eileen O'Donnell, Julia Oliver, Robert Osborne, James Parish, Taylor Pero, Steven Rebello, William & Ann Relling Jr., Joe Richards, Steve Rogers, Coyne Steven Sanders, Jack Scovil, Dave Smith, Bob Taylor (Lincoln Center Library), Brenda Thomson, Robert Tieman, Richard Vasquez, Suzanne Weed, Cathy and Randy Wharton, Will Willoughby, Jo Anne Worley & Roger Perry, and Lucy Zakhary.

To J. Randy Taraborrelli who first said, "This is good, Rich!" (and never changed his mind). Enormous thanks to the always generous and gracious Dorris Halsey, and her associate Kimberley Cameron. Also to Noel Young, David Dahl and Frank Goad at Capra Press.

Finally, a special note of gratitude to Mr. Billy Barnes. Without Billy's love, support, patience, consideration and respect, this book may never have metamorphosed from thought to form.

Introduction

by Jerry Herman

RUTH HERMAN, my mom, was beautiful, talented and glamorous and saw to it that I grew up in a home overflowing with warmth and laughter. Sound familiar? So it's no wonder that I thought about her that first day I began working on the score for *Mame*; that awful moment when all you have are sharpened pencils, blank paper and a freshly tuned Steinway staring back at you. I wanted to get the opening number out of the way. It had to take place at a huge party, and party songs are usually a bore to write and a bore to listen to. But, lightning struck. I remembered coming home from school one day and finding my mother surrounded by hors d'oeuvres. It was a Tuesday or a Thursday in the middle of the winter and I remembered asking, "What's the occasion?" She flashed me a smile and said, "It's today!" I had my song, and so much more. I realized that my own mother was the best reference point for Mame I could possibly imagine. The score simply poured out of me.

And so each step of our journey to the Winter Garden Theatre became more joyous, more incredible. The five week rehearsal period flew by – even Philadelphia was memorable. Larry Gelbart once wrote, "If Hitler were alive today, I'd wish he were out-of-town with a Broadway musical!" The horror stories of people's experiences during those tense, panic-filled weeks before the opening of a major new musical compare only to tales of the Spanish Inquisition!

Well, not so with us. I went to the movies with Angela

Lansbury and Bea Arthur during the out-of-town tryout of *Mame!* It's not supposed to be like that, is it?

At the orchestra run through, Angie and I were awash in boxes of Kleenex as we cheered Phil Lang's orchestrations and Don Pippin's crisp and sensitive conducting. The first preview, though overlong and tentative, told us in no uncertain terms that there was a smash on that stage.

The next day, Director Gene Saks told us that our major work was to cut thirty minutes, and he proposed we do it slowly and gently in order not to harm the fabric of the piece. And so every day, a sliver of dialogue or a snippet of song was dropped, so that by the time we left Philly the show had strengthened and clarified without the usual sturm and drang. I know it's not supposed to be like that!

We shopped at Wanamakers and dined at Bookbinders. One Sunday afternoon at the venerable seafood establishment, we ordered drinks, only to be squelched by a little, mustached waiter who seemed annoyed that we had forgotten that Philadelphia blue laws allowed no alcohol sold on the first day of the week. Someone at the table whispered a rumor that for special clientele the restaurant had been known to serve drinks on Sunday in white ceramic mugs with teaspoons in them, so that from the sidewalk it would look like a tea party was going on inside. When the waiter returned for our food order, Bea Arthur, in her most resonant baritone, bellowed at the little man, "Tell Mr. Bookbinder to bring me a cup of vodka!" The restaurant came apart at the seams. It's definitely not supposed to be like that!

On opening night, on my way to the Winter Garden, a record shop was blasting Bobby Darin's single of the title song and Eydie Gorme's gorgeous rendition of "If He Walked Into My Life." The airwaves were so full of both songs that they both received recognition applause during the overture. The performance was smooth and secure and the ovation that Angie received at the curtain call shook the very foundations of the great house. A few hours later Angie and I swept across the vast circular dance floor of the Rainbow Room to our table, and the cheering was deafening.

So what better time is there for me to say thank you for the grandest theatrical experience of them all. Thank you to Angie, Bea, Jane and Frankie, Gene, Onna, Bob and the Eckarts, Sylvia, Bobby, Jimmy and John, Don and Phil...and especially to Lawrence and Lee and Patrick Dennis. Thank you for giving me a non-stop, life-long, glorious party called *Mame*.

How my mom would have loved it.

– JERRY HERMAN
Beverly Hills, California

Preface

BUT DARLING, I'M YOUR AUNTIE MAME! is the amazing story of how one outrageous, fascinating, larger-than-life but extraordinarily human fictional character changed the course of numerous theatrical careers and became one of the most popular heroines to ever grace the pages of two novels, two stage plays and two sparkling screen adaptations. Indeed, Auntie Mame is no less than an American icon in literature and entertainment.

This is the never-before-told tale of Broadway and Hollywood's Golden Ages; of an effervescent and unforgettable literary creation once described as possessing the best features of Tallulah Bankhead, the Duchess of Windsor, Cinderella – and a touch of Princess Diana tossed in for good measure. This indomitable force of nature continues to delight the world with her simple – but profound – philosophy of life: "Live! Life is a banquet, and most poor sons-of-bitches are starving to death!"[1]– even if the sanitized 1958 screen version had her instead retort, "Most poor *suckers* are starving to death!"

In January 1955, Vanguard Press in New York published what they thought was an amusing trifle in the form of a 280-page novel titled, *Auntie Mame*, written by relatively unknown author, Patrick Dennis. It was a satirical and witty story about a rather unusual character: a wealthy eccentric who suddenly and unexpectedly inherits her 10-year-old nephew and proceeds to show him – by her irrepressible free-spirited example – the

---

[1] That line, written by Jerome Lawreence & Robert E. Lee, was never in Patrick Dennis' book, but only in the play and musical.

15

unlimited possibilities of life in the proverbial big city; the deflating of pretentiousness; and even the fighting of prejudice – always with wit, style, warmth and wisdom.

Within weeks of its publication, the book (subtitled *An Irreverent Escapade*), was the talk of the nation. As readers cackled about the outlandish situations and philosophies of this kooky eccentric, critics babbled praise for the liberated, unconventional – and some said off-her-rocker – Mame, irrevocably christening her one of the most unique and unlikely of literary heroines.

In quick succession, the book landed on the *New York Times* best-seller list (February 20, 1955) and was immediately optioned for dramatization for the stage, destined to become one of Broadway's longest-running comedies, giving motion picture star Rosalind Russell not only her greatest theatrical triumph, but also the most identifiable characterization of a career that spanned four decades.

The phenomenal success of Jerome Lawrence & Robert E. Lee's play *Auntie Mame* led to the equally successful multi-Academy Award-nominated Warner Bros. 1958 movie also star-ring Russell – a film that, according to Clive Hirschhorn in his history of the studio, *The Warner Bros. Story*, virtually rescued the studio from oncoming bankruptcy the year of its release.

A sequel to the novel, *Around the World With Auntie Mame*, (dedicated to Rosalind Russell) was published in 1957 and it too instantly became a best-seller. And, despite the initial pes-simism of a few, Auntie Mame proved to be much more durable than a novelty or short-term curiosity.

The world's burgeoning love affair with this bodacious, fun-lov-ing madcap hit even greater heights when the Lawrence & Lee/Jerry Herman musical *Mame* opened at the Winter Garden Theatre in New York on May 24, 1966. Hailed by critics as "The best musical of the season," star Angela Lansbury, as the colorful and now musical *Mame* – with Beatrice Arthur as her best friend and cohort Vera Charles – won Tony Awards for best performances by an actress and supporting actress, respectively, in a Broadway musical that year. The play – which introduced the show-stopping title song, "Mame" and the contemporary standards, "We Need a Little Christmas," "Bosom Buddies," "Open a New Window" and "If He Walked Into My Life" – ran for a remarkable five years.

With innumerable road companies of both the play *Auntie Mame* and the musical *Mame* running simultaneously around the world, Patrick Dennis' character became a household name and 20th century classic within a relatively short period of time. Almost from the beginning, one could hardly remember a time when an Auntie Mame wasn't a euphemism for a wacky but lovable, wealthy dilettante.

With the great success of the two novels, the stage and Hollywood versions of *Auntie Mame* and the blockbuster status of the musical *Mame* on Broadway, it was inevitable that another movie based on the material would emerge. In 1974, Mame was reincarnated, this time starring the world's most popular redhead – Lucille Ball.

*

Far from being identified with just one or two legendary Broadway and motion picture stars however, this unlikely heroine – making for an irresistible tour-de-force for many female stars over age forty – has become an annuity of sorts for some of the entertainment industry's most venerable talents: Greer Garson, Beatrice Lillie, Constance Bennett, Janet Blair, Janis Paige, Elaine Stritch, Gisele MacKenzie, Ann Miller, Celeste Holm, Shirl Conway, Sylvia Sidney, Eve Arden, Ann Southern, Jan Sterling, Gretchen Wyler, Jane Morgan, Jo Anne Worley, Jan Clayton, Juliet Prowse, Mariette Hartley, Ginger Rogers, Gypsy Rose Lee, Patrice Munsel, Susan Hayward, Alexis Smith and Carole Cook (who starred in both the play and musical), on down to Morgan Brittany, to name just a few.

17

Translated into more than 30 languages, *Auntie Mame*, and the musical *Mame*, have never ceased being performed somewhere in the world almost every evening since their respective Broadway debuts in 1956 and 1966. Foreign stars in the role include Spain's Conchita Montes; Berthe Quistgaard in the Lars Schmidt (Ingrid Bergman's husband) production in Denmark, Gaelae Byrne in Australia, Sylvia Pinal for two years in Mexico, two separate *Mame* productions and stars in Japan, and Lilebil Ibsen (Henrik Ibsen's granddaughter).

But Darling, I'm Your Auntie Mame! (Mame's theatrically effusive greeting to her awestruck little nephew Patrick), is a chronicle of how it all *really* began. When Patrick Dennis slipped that first piece of paper into his typewriter and began tapping out the saga of Mame Dennis, he could not know that he was about to create a national institution and a character whose popularity will never diminish.

As writer Omar Ranney of *Stage and Screen Magazine* proclaimed, "The entire civilized world has heard of Auntie Mame. In fact, it would not be surprising if the savage tribes of the earth's most remote corners heard about her too."

But Darling, I'm Your Auntie Mame! is the fascinating and – like Mame herself – the larger-than-life story of how it all began – and, most probably, how it will never end.

And finally, a caution: There should not be any problem in *context*, but the reader should be alert to the fact that, as noted, the novel, stageplay and film of the play all have the same title, *Auntie Mame*. The Broadway musical and movie of the musical are also similarly titled *Mame*. See appendices for cast lists of the original productions as a furthur guide. Thank you.

– RICHARD TYLER JORDAN
Los Angeles, California

CHAPTER ONE

Auntie Mame On Broadway

IN THE MID-1950'S, Broadway was still enjoying its brilliantly inventive post World War II renaissance. Despite the encroachment of the increasingly popular medium of television, theatre audiences continued to flock to New York for a dazzling array of musicals, comedies and dramas.

With the lure of such first-rate attractions as *My Fair Lady* starring Julie Andrews and Rex Harrison, Frank Loesser's *The Most Happy Fella*, *Mr. Wonderful* with Sammy Davis, Jr., *The Great Sebastians* starring Alfred Lunt and Lynn Fontaine, Eugene O'Neill's *Long Day's Journey Into Night*, and Jerome Lawrence & Robert E. Lee's classic courtroom drama *Inherit the Wind*, Broadway was still a top draw for sophisticated, superbly mounted entertainment, despite the fact that theatre ticket prices were becoming outrageously high – $6.90 for Friday and Saturday night performances.

Soon after Vanguard Press published Patrick Dennis' third novel *Auntie Mame: An Irreverent Escapade*, in January 1955, Broadway producers Robert Fryer and Lawrence ("Jimmy") Carr realized the enormous potential for a stage dramatization of the book.

With the smash Betty Comden & Adolph Green/Leonard Bernstein Broadway musical hit *Wonderful Town* starring Rosalind Russell already under Robert Fryer's producing belt (for which he and Russell both won Tony Awards), as well as William Merchant's *The Desk Set* (starring Shirley Booth), produced with Carr, the two producers had become important figures in the New York theatre scene.

It was Sunday morning, January 23. With eyes always on the lookout for potential theatrical properties, the duo began their weekly ritual of examining the Sunday *New York Times'* Book Review supplement for synopses of new publications. On this overcast, winter morning, literary critic Ben Crisler's review of *Auntie Mame* appeared, and Carr was immediately intrigued by the story's flamboyant heroine. Though the synopsis was far from a rave, Carr was excited by the main character as described by Crisler. He showed the column to Fryer. It read:

"If this strange book should turn out to be a best-seller (as seems entirely possible), it will not be because it is as sweetly idealistic as *I Remember Mama* or as delightfully wholesome as *The Egg and I*. In fact, Mr. Dennis' left-handed tribute to the alleged aunt who, from his tenth year, provided him with a home influence as eccentric as any lad ever fell heir to, raises a serious question whether one should be kind to orphans, especially to the point of adoption."

After reading the article – which included a brief storyline summation – Fryer agreed with Carr's positive evaluation of it as a possible theatrical property – possibly serving as a stage vehicle for renowned Broadway and motion picture star Shirley Booth, with whom they had just concluded working on the hit comedy *The Desk Set*.

That same afternoon, Robert Fryer and Jimmy Carr left their Rumson, New Jersey home on a mission – to find a copy of *Auntie Mame*. Fryer remembers that his partner was the first to read the book and was wildly enthusiastic about both the story, and the eccentric Mame Dennis character: a lady of means who belongs to the Algonquin literary set in 1928 New York, thrives on cocktail parties and fads and who suddenly becomes the guardian of her 10-year-old nephew.

While reading *Auntie Mame* that same day, Jimmy Carr felt what actress Rosalind Russell later wrote in a published review of the paperback edition of the novel: "*Auntie Mame* has a lot in common with those literary heroines of earlier years – Scarlett O'Hara, Lorelei Lee and Blanche Dubois. Mame could match wisecracks with Lorelei any day. Her manipulation of men would put Scarlett out of the running in the first heat. And she could rattle off more Freudian psychology than Blanche could pick up in a lifetime of psychotherapy. Yet Mame has one saving grace that none of these intense ladies possesses – a devastating, totally irreverent sense of humor."

Auntie Mame enchanted young producer Carr, and he insisted that his colleague call the publisher immediately the next morning to obtain the name of the author's agent.

As Vanguard Press opened for business that Monday morning, January 24, Fryer telephoned editor-in-chief Julian Muller, who had discovered, nurtured and edited *Auntie Mame*. He informed Fryer that Elizabeth Otis of the McIntosh/Otis Literary Agency was Dennis' representative but that stage and film rights to the book were being handled by top agent Annie Laurie Williams.

A legendary name in literary representation, Annie Laurie Williams was most noted for negotiating the sale of Margaret Mitchell's classic American Civil War epic *Gone With the Wind* to motion picture producer David O. Selznick. During her durable and illustrious career she represented many great books and their revered authors including John Steinbeck (*The Grapes of Wrath*), Kathleen Windsor (*Forever Amber*), Lloyd C. Douglas (*The Magnificent Obsession*) and, later, Truman Capote.

When Fryer reached Williams by phone, he introduced himself and asked if the dramatic rights to *Auntie Mame* were available. Williams was of course familiar with Fryer's burgeoning

Broadway reputation and told him the dramatization rights were indeed available, but added that a number of other people were interested and, in fact, were already placing bids. Furthermore, she planned to close a deal "immediately."

An anxious Robert Fryer asked her to delay any commitments for one day, promising Williams that he and his partner would be in her office Tuesday morning to discuss the details of *their* buying the dramatic rights. He stayed up most of that Monday night reading what the *Chicago Tribune* called "the funniest story about the most unforgettable character you'll ever run across."

"I laughed hysterically," Fryer recalls of the first time he read *Auntie Mame*. He was also greatly moved by the story, and his intuition affirmed that a successful play could be gleaned from the book. "I'm Mr. Average Audience," he demurs. "If something moves me to either laughter or tears, I know it's right." Fryer was convinced that he and Carr were about to be part of something very special.

The following morning the two producers met at Annie Laurie Williams' 18 East 41st Street office. After relatively brief negotiations, Fryer and Carr signed a contract, shook hands with Williams and walked away with the prize – the dramatic rights to what would become one of the top 100 longest-running Broadway plays in history and a motion picture classic.

It had been a whirlwind of activities for the producing team. In just three short days, they had gone from being two producers in search of another project, to the owners of what was quickly becoming the most talked-about book of the year and a classic of modern literature.

By the time *Auntie Mame* climbed aboard the *New York Times'* best-sellers list, where it would remain for over 2 years (112 weeks), they had purchased the rights to adapt the story for stage and screen. They felt that they were on the very threshold of something unique and were eager to find the right combination of star, director and writer.

After reading *Auntie Mame* again and earnestly discussing it at length, Fryer and Carr agreed that the title character sounded more like legendary comedienne Beatrice Lillie, or possibly even their friend Rosalind Russell, than original candidate Shirley Booth. Fryer had remained extremely close with Hollywood film legend and multi-Oscar nominee Russell, ever since her triumphant appearances as the star of Fryer's 1953 Broadway production of *Wonderful Town*. He immediately telephoned her to discuss *Auntie Mame*.

From her film debut in 1934, Rosalind Russell was deemed one of the most popular, if not preeminent, screen stars of Hollywood. During the so-called "Golden Age" of movies, Russell was no less than a bona-fide "great lady of the silver screen," a tribute still paid to the late actress. However, by the time *Auntie Mame* appeared in print, Russell's career had begun to stagnate and she was seeking a new direction and focus. By Hollywood's standards of youth, she was practically over the hill, and she desperately needed something to rejuvenate her marquee magic.

"I didn't mind that my box office was dropping," Russell later insisted. "What I did mind were the doubts being cast on my ability as an actress." She had in fact, aimed for the stage since childhood.

Born at home in Waterbury, Connecticut, June 4, 1911, to James Edward Russell, a lawyer, and his wife Clara McKnight, Rosalind Knight Russell was the fourth of seven children, "The ham in the middle," she was fond of saying.

She attended Marymount College at Tarrytown-on-the-Hudson and then enrolled at the American Academy of Dramatic Arts in New York. After graduation and appearing in numerous stage shows in Boston and New York, Russell made her Broadway debut in 1930, in "Garrick Gaieties" at the Guild

Theatre. She went on to win a Hollywood screen test and a long term contract at Metro Goldwyn Mayer, before starring in her first feature film "Evelyn Prentice," in 1934.

Known to be a shrewd businesswoman, Russell was one of the first stars to break away from the contract system to become an independent player in Hollywood. In 1943, she was the highest-paid actress in films, reportedly commanding $250,000 per film. (During a career that spanned nearly 40 years and over 50 feature motion pictures, some of her more memorable films include: *The Women* (1939), *His Girl Friday* (1940), *My Sister Eileen* (1942), *Take a Letter, Darling* (1942), *Picnic* (1955) and *Five Finger Exercise* (1962).

During her reign as a Hollywood superstar, Rosalind Russell was nominated for the Academy Award four times (*My Sister Eileen*, 1942; *Sister Kenny*, 1946; *Mourning Becomes Electra*, 1947; and *Auntie Mame*, 1958); but the coveted statuette was never presented to the star for her acting. However, in 1973 she did receive the icon in the guise of the Jean Hersholt Humanitarian Award, in recognition of her outstanding support of numerous charitable causes including serving as the national co-chair of the Arthritis and Rheumatism Foundation, and her work on behalf of Sister Elizabeth Kenny's polio clinic.

The end of her life was filled with pain and sickness. Crippling rheumatoid arthritis and cancer ravaged her body and she was confined to Cedars of Lebanon Hospital in Los Angeles for nearly three months before she died Sunday morning, November 28, 1976. As Frank Sinatra said in his eulogy for the star, "Our Lord got up and said, 'Better send for Roz ... she's suffered enough.'"

*

In later newspaper accounts, as well as in her posthumously published 1977 autobiography, *Life Is a Banquet* (written with

Rosalind Russell as she appeared in an MGM publicity photo circa 1935
(Author's collection)

Chris Chase), Russell insisted that it was *she* who bought the rights to the *Auntie Mame* novel after author Patrick Dennis sent her the typewritten unpublished manuscript with a note stating: "You are my Auntie Mame for stage and screen." In her book, Russell wrote that it was she who convinced producers Fryer and Carr to assemble the play for her as a star vehicle: "Yes, I bought the book all right, and I'm going to open it in New York at the Broadhurst Theatre early in November 1956. I'm hoping to get Garson Kanin to direct it. He'd be just right."

By all accounts, however, Russell was in Connecticut staying with her sister – resting between motion picture commitments – when Robert Fryer telephoned to discuss the literary property that *he* had just purchased.

Russell had recently completed filming the musical, *The Girl Rush,* – Paramount Pictures's attempt to cash in on Roz's Broadway triumph as a musical comedy performer in *Wonderful Town* – and was shortly to report to the Saline, Nebraska, location set for the Columbia Pictures production of Joshua Logan's *Picnic.* On the phone with Russell, Fryer expressed his enthusiasm about his recent acquisition of *Auntie Mame*, telling her that he had an extremely funny book that he felt would make an equally funny stage play. He urged Roz to read it and consider portraying the character on Broadway; intrigued, she asked him to immediately send the book to her in Connecticut.

Too anxious to wait for the mail delivery, Fryer and his partner drove to Connecticut from New Jersey to personally deliver the book to the star. In tow was noted novelist/playwright Sumner Locke Elliott, who they decided should fashion the stage dramatization of the book.

"We were invited for tea," Elliott recalls of that afternoon in Connecticut with Russell. "Almost immediately I realized that everybody, including Fryer and Carr, were going to be absolute putty in her hands. Miss Russell was a formidable thing. She was a triumphantly big, important movie star. I hadn't been involved with that kind of Hollywood personality before.

"From the very beginning, Bobby [Fryer] said, 'We *must* get Roz to do the play, and getting Roz isn't going to be easy.' I imagined this to mean that I must be very careful in what I said, and must not go against her in any way; at least not in the beginning, until we had heard her out."

The producers described the story to Russell. She countered with her own ideas about the plot and how it should be manipulated on stage. Elliott remembers that one of the first things Russell said was, "I don't want to do this thing set in the 1920s. I don't want to be wearing those silly hats and doing the kinds of things that Carol Channing does [in *Gentlemen Prefer Blondes*]!"

As Elliott astutely notes, "One of the important sub-plots in the book is the Wall Street stock market crash of the 1920s. Taking that away would rob the story of much of its humor and original intent."

The creative triumvirate from New York sat and patiently listened to the fading Hollywood star pontificate about how everything in the show must be "totally up to date." Russell cited the success in Boston of her producer/husband Frederick Brisson's musical *Damn Yankees* as the perfect example of a contemporary star vehicle. "That show's a smash because it's absolutely up to date," she exclaimed. "It has *nothing* whatsoever to do with the *boring twenties*!"

Elliott also remembers that Russell had primed her sister before the meeting to go along with her notion about changes in the story. "This is how sly she was. Her sister had been out while we were discussing the project. When she arrived back, Roz said to her, 'Now here's a big secret, I might be doing

Auntie Mame on Broadway.' Her sister remarked, 'How wonderful! I hear that it's marvelously funny, but oh, dear, I wish it wasn't set in the 1920s and you didn't have to wear those silly hats like Carol Channing does!' To which Roz cracked, 'There you have it! That's exactly what I'm saying! We cannot do this thing in the '20s.'"

In a barbed aside to his cohorts, Fryer remarked sarcastically, "We almost needn't have bought the book."

And, as Elliott recalls, "By the time we left that afternoon, I said to myself, this project should be called *Auntie Roz!*"

It was only a hint of what was to come.

CHAPTER TWO

Getting Roz

PRIVATELY, ROSALIND RUSSELL read *Auntie Mame* and was charged with enthusiasm for what she politely told the producers might "possibly" make a good vehicle for her next Broadway venture. But, in order to strengthen her bargaining position with these producers who obviously coveted her for the role – she coquettishly told them it was "far too early" for her to commit to an unscripted play. She agreed to reconsider when a script was available for her evaluation.

Russell's sharp business sense served her well. Though she refused to commit to Fryer and Carr, she, however, immediately perceived the vast potential the *Auntie Mame* property promised her; she in fact confided to her close friend, actor/photographer Cris Alexander at this early juncture, that she was indeed very excited about the potential project.

Alexander recalls, "I was in *Wonderful Town* with Rosalind and we became really thick friends. She called me after reading *Auntie Mame* and said, 'I have gotten a hold of the most wonderful property I've ever read in my life.' Rosalind later told me that before she got halfway through reading the book she said to herself, 'I have *got* to do this!'"

As intuitive as Russell was about the potential for this property, she nevertheless needed the support of a trusted advisor. She presented a copy of *Auntie Mame* to her friend (and future *Picnic* director) Joshua Logan. When he finished reading the book, Logan agreed that it could be quite a good project for the brunette comedienne; it certainly had all the elements of characters and interesting situations that he regarded as crucial for a good play.

Yet, Russell still stalled in making a decision and would not pledge to be Auntie Mame on stage, even as columnists insisted that she was "nearly" signed to star in the stage dramatization of the now best-selling Patrick Dennis book.

Robert Fryer was anxious for the rumors about Russell's participation to become a reality, inundating her with copies of the best reviews of the book to keep her interest piqued. He also stayed in constant touch with the star, expressing his continued eagerness to somehow work out contract details.

"The whole project and the idea of working with you is so stimulating and exciting, and the possibility of the book yielding a very excellent play," he effusively wrote, "I don't think anything should be allowed to mar it."

As Patrick Dennis' book continued to climb the nation's best-seller lists, Fryer and Carr weren't the only Broadway producers to see the possibilities of adapting the book for the stage. Frederick Brisson, producer of such legendary musicals as *The Pajama Game* and *Damn Yankees* – and, not coincidentally, Rosalind Russell's husband – was equally intrigued by the story of the madcap aunt, especially as a star vehicle for his wife. According to one source involved in the production, Brisson wanted very much to be a member of the team bringing this project to fruition. Fryer and Carr however, were adamantly opposed to working with him. Undeterred, Brisson was so unabashed in his bid to join the duo that he "disclosed" in a newspaper item that he was indeed co-producing *Auntie Mame* with Fryer and Carr.

When news of that column item reached the producers, the two were incensed. They stated flatly, in fact, that there was no way they were going to share producing credits with Brisson. Fryer even demanded a retraction of the column item. At the same time he explained that although he and Carr were negotiating for Russell, they were still far apart on contractual terms. He shrewdly announced that Russell was by no means the only star under consideration for the plum role.

Reportedly, at the time, an agitated Robert Fryer telephoned Rosalind Russell and angrily stipulated, "If he's [Brisson] part of this show, you're not doing it for us. We own the rights!" He capped this by pointedly telling her that international music hall sensation Beatrice Lillie might play Auntie Mame brilliantly.

Brisson now had little choice but to abandon any formal involvement in the production. He sulked away, but he did however participate actively as much as he could in the behind-the-scenes pre-production of *Auntie Mame*.

Though Frederick Brisson was no longer *officially* connected with *Auntie Mame* in any capacity except that of the potential star's husband, he remained fervently interested in the project – if only to protect his wife's proposed financial investment in the show. If and when she agreed to do the role, she intended to be the play's principal investor. "I'd learned about the benefits of ownership from *Wonderful Town*," Russell said in her autobiography. "In *Wonderful Town* I took a lot of money, all salary, and most of it went to Uncle Sam. This time I was willing to settle for less salary, but I wanted a piece of the action."

While coaxing Rosalind Russell to star in the play, Fryer and Carr simultaneously discussed candidates for director, the leading contender being Morton ("Tec" – pronounced "Teek") DaCosta, whose stage credits up to that time included such hits as *Plain and Fancy* and the comedy *No Time For Sergeants*.

DaCosta recalls that he and Russell both eventually agreed to do the play based upon enjoying the Patrick Dennis book and believing a good play could ultimately be gleaned from it. "Roz and I signed contracts at practically the same time," he recalls.

"I was in Europe when I received a telephone call from Bobby Fryer asking if I would be interested in directing Rosalind Russell in *Auntie Mame*."

Russell's book again describes a different scenario, stating that she picked the director on the basis of seeing his Broadway comedy hit *No Time For Sergeants*. Writing in her memoirs about the subject, Russell stated: "When I came out of the theatre after seeing *No Time For Sergeants*, I turned to Bobby Fryer. 'What's the name of the guy who did this?'

'Morton DaCosta,' said Bobby.

'That's the director I want,' I said.

Bobby was startled. 'Roz, you didn't even laugh.'

'I don't like toilet jokes,' I said. 'But this guy took a book and made it play on stage. He's had a couple of nice hits, now he's ready for a smash, a real smash, and he'll be eager to work.' Never have I been more clever."

That recollection seems a bit far-fetched. Most likely, Russell had read the *Playbill* handed to her as she entered the theatre, the text of which would have familiarized her with the biographies of all the principal creative people involved in the production. Indeed, she was also on the prowl for a potential director for her own show. And, she contradicted her innocence about the director and his reputation by acknowledging, "He's had a couple of nice hits."

DaCosta's memory of the genesis of his involvement is quite different: "That story in her book is a lot of nonsense," he said. "I had known Bobby [Fryer] for a long time and he sent me a copy of *Auntie Mame* while I was in London, and from enjoying the book I agreed to direct the play. We didn't even have a script then. I came back to the States and went out to the Coast to meet with Roz, to kick the character around and see how she thought it should be delineated. Rosalind was so bright. She always had input in everything that she did and I'm very instruction-conscious, so we both plowed away at it."

As there was still no script for the *Auntie Mame* play at this juncture, it had been difficult for the producers to barter for the services of DaCosta and Russell. But a good story was certainly there in the book, and everyone agreed it had potential for the stage. Now, finding a suitable playwright to successfully dramatize the series of vignettes of which the book was comprised faced them and proved to be one of the toughest challenges of this or any other Broadway venture.

Early on, Fryer and Carr had carefully considered numerous writers, eventually selecting Sumner Locke Elliott. Fryer had known Elliott since their early days in television when the producer had been a casting director, and Elliott was writing for such successful live programs as *Studio One*, *Playhouse 90* and *Philco Playhouse*. Elliott's agent, Annie Laurie Williams, convinced Fryer and Carr that her client would be the right talent to adapt *Auntie Mame* for the stage.

The Australian-born immigrant whose varied artistic career included success as an actor, novelist and playwright, Elliott had achieved Broadway fame as a writer several seasons earlier with his play *John Murry Anderson's Almanac* as well as 1951's *Buy Me Blue Ribbons*.

"Quite frankly, I was not absolutely wild about the *Auntie Mame* book," confides Elliott. "I didn't think it was as funny as everybody else thought it was. Privately, it wasn't quite my cup of tea, and I wish now that I had turned the producers down at the start because the whole situation became rather unhappy for me, from beginning to end. Fortunately, I had it in my contract that if after the first draft I didn't want to pursue the project I could withdraw."

After that initial meeting in Connecticut with Russell and the producers, Elliott was left with the prospect of writing a script based on whatever Miss Russell wanted. Although he thought her whole approach was completely wrong – and that it was unfair to Patrick Dennis and to his book – he conceded that he was being paid to perform a duty. He decided to do as he was told for the first draft, and after that, perhaps he could refashion the script to adhere to the original intent of the story.

Elliott sequestered himself for six weeks in a farmhouse in New Jersey, writing his first draft of *Auntie Mame* – but knowing all the while that it was completely wrong. "The changes that Roz wanted had nothing to do with the book," he laments. "For instance, she had it all being done in one set, and she had cut out all the Southern characters including the whole Beauregard Burnside incident. It was a desecration!"

Robert Fryer, however, remained optimistic – at least in his reports to Russell. "I really think, after his [Elliott's] play outline, that if the actual writing is as good as his plot structure, we'll have something awfully good." As Fryer wrote to Russell about Elliott just before she left for Kansas and the filming of *Picnic*, "I am so hopeful that *Auntie Mame* will turn out well. And it should, the 'bones' are there and I think something good will develop."

By June 1955, an apparently confident Sumner Locke Elliott reported to Fryer and Carr that *Auntie Mame* was "practically writing itself." An ecstatic Fryer contacted Russell with a progress report and passed on Elliott's feelings that *Auntie Mame* had turned out to be a "wonderful project" and that he was getting all her "marvelous characteristics." He added, "She is warm, human, funny and has a great deal of courage."

But Elliott refused to delude himself. "I knew all along that it was in terrible trouble," he now concedes.

Fryer was convinced that they would have Elliott's first draft by the beginning of July and informed Russell that upon receipt he would forward it to Beverly Hills for her comments. Accepting the fact that there would inevitably be much work to do on the play once Elliott had turned in his first effort, the producers' only thoughts were to get the character down on paper with a good basic story structure.

But as the rainy spring of 1955 graduated into a humid New York summer, Elliott submitted his work to Fryer and Carr; and the aghast reaction of the producers confirmed the playwright's worst apprehensions.

In addition to Fryer and Carr, Patrick Dennis and his agent Elisabeth Otis read the Elliott script. "They were absolutely appalled at the content," Elliott candidly admits.

A meeting was hastily called to discuss the debacle. In addition to Sumner Locke Elliott, those present at the assembly included Robert Fryer and Patrick Dennis' agent and lawyer.

"The meeting went on for about an hour, and I was subjected to much intense questioning about why this had happened," Elliott remembers. "Of course it all happened because of Miss Russell. It was all her doing. But nobody was allowed to say *one word* against her because she was sacred. Since she still had not signed to do the play the producers were afraid she might turn it down completely if she was criticized. So the whole affair was almost iniquitous. I suddenly said, 'I'm not going to do this! I don't think there's any reason to go on with this conversation. I'm going to exercise my right and contractually give up the adaptation!'

"Nobody stood up for me, not even Bobby Fryer, whom I considered my friend. He would not say a word in my defense to explain why a Hollywood actress could dictate the terms of how a Broadway play should be written.

"They [Fryer and Carr] should have known that her career

was in trouble and that *Auntie Mame* was going to be the thing that rescued her from almost the end of her career. But instead, they allowed her to wind them around her little finger."

As Sumner Locke Elliott departed, the worried producers began a desperate search for another writer.

On September 9, 1955, the New York *Times* announced that the plum assignment of adapting *Auntie Mame* for the stage had been passed to Patrick Dennis himself. It seemed a logical choice as Dennis was considered one of the wittiest, most perceptive and insightful writers of the day and, furthermore, Auntie Mame was his character. The *Times* also hinted that there was talk of turning the property into a musical comedy. However, that idea was not seriously considered – for another eight years.

October 1955 was an auspicious month for both Fryer and Carr and the Brissons. En route to England aboard the Queen Elizabeth II, for the London West End opening of Brisson's musical *Damn Yankees*, Rosalind and Freddie stopped in New York long enough to meet once again with the producers. At this point the star finally agreed to accept their offer to star in *Auntie Mame.* However, everyone involved pledged not to announce their contract until the following February, by which time a draft of the play was expected.

Though it has since been vehemently denied by Robert Fryer, the pact for Russell's services at least *verbally* included Frederick Brisson as a producer. As inducement for Russell to agree to do *Auntie Mame,* Fryer had apparently relented in his earlier decision about sharing producing chores with Brisson.

"Jimmy and I want you to do the play and the picture," Fryer stated in writing, "and we want Freddie to do the play with us, so you are protected. We just have to get a good play out of the whole thing and we'll all be very happy."

In retrospect it appears that the producers wanted Roz so badly they were willing to concede to almost any of her demands to obtain her signature on a contract. They may not have really wanted Brisson's name attached to the credits, but they were willing to say anything in order to secure her commitment.

"Jimmy and I are of course delighted that you and Freddie will be with us on *Auntie Mame*," Fryer wrote to Russell while she was in England. "It is a hard nut to crack," he said of getting all the elements of the play together, "but I think with four of us working on it plus the author, and a good director, we should lick it. No word will get out, of course, from us, until you approve the script. Tanner (Patrick Dennis) will have one ready by November 1. You will be great in the role. We are also extremely happy to have Freddie with us as we not only like him so much as a friend, but also respect his business acumen."

In another letter from Robert Fryer to Rosalind Russell, dated October 31, 1955 – exactly one year to the day from the eventual opening of *Auntie Mame* on Broadway – he stated, "We received the first draft of *Auntie Mame* from Tanner this week so if you return [from London] next week it will be ready for you. Jimmy and I feel we will definitely need a writer/director to work with Pat [Tanner]. However, these are all things we will talk about next week when you get back."

By the time Russell returned to the States, the producers felt more than a little grim about the script that had been handed to them. Russell confirmed their worst fears when she read the manuscript, declaring in no uncertain terms that she was completely dissatisfied with it and would not do it as written.

Vanguard's editor-in-chief Julian Muller remembers that Patrick Dennis' script was not without merit, but it was painfully obvious that Dennis just wasn't a playwright – and he knew it.

Dennis' attempt at adapting his own book was completely

unacceptable to the star and producers – a rambling text of uninspired and amazingly unfunny pages of dialogue. It was said (in jest), that after 500 pages had issued from Dennis' old gray Royal typewriter, Fryer inquired about how the play was coming along. Dennis responded dryly, "Fine. I'm nearly finished – with the first act."

It was now December, 1955 and though everyone involved was still more or less interested in the project, the most important element of the play was still missing – a script. When Brisson and Russell returned to Beverly Hills that month, they took it upon themselves to seek a suitable author.

It was now nearly a year after Fryer and Carr had first obtained the dramatic rights for the book, and Frederick Brisson sent telegrams to nearly every writer of note that he and his wife could collectively think of, asking: WOULD YOU BE AVAILABLE AND INTERESTED IN DRAMATIZING AUNTIE MAME TO STAR ROZ FOR BROADWAY. SHOW TO GO INTO PRODUCTION NO LATER THAN SEPTEMBER.

Their lofty wish list of authors included such giants as Cole Porter (which would have been a creative departure for the brilliant songwriter), Irwin Shaw, Moss Hart, Arthur Laurents, Noël Coward and Truman Capote. For various and individual reasons, however, none of these *name writers* would commit to the project.

One of the so-called *literati* to whom the Brisson's solicited services for adapting the book was F. Hugh Herbert, perhaps best described as the Neil Simon of his day.

Born in 1897, Herbert was regarded as a prolific screenwriter, Broadway playwright and author of short stories and novels. Beginning with the 1926 silent film *The Waning Sex*, Herbert's numerous feature film writing credits included *Adam and Evil* (1927), *The Cardboard Lover* (1928), *X Marks the Spot* (1931), *Vanity Fair* (1932), *The Constant Woman* (1934), *Home Sweet*

Homicide (1946) and *For Love or Money* (1958). His screen adaptation of his own play, *The Moon Is Blue* (1953) was a *cause célèbre* in the 1950s for its then-daring use of the word "virgin," in defiance of the Catholic Legion of Decency and the censorship code.

Brisson sent a copy of *Auntie Mame* to Herbert's Bel Air, California, home in late 1955, with a letter requesting that he read the book and comment on the possibility of tackling a stage adaptation. Though *Auntie Mame* was the country's #1 best-selling work of fiction, when Herbert finished the tome, he sent off an immediate and carefully worded reply to Brisson, stating how much he *hated* the story and how *appalled* he was that anyone would want to expose this character on a Broadway stage.

Herbert was shocked by *Auntie Mame*. He advised Brisson that as an ardent and long-time admirer of Rosalind Russell, he was deeply concerned that she was even considering portraying such a "despicable" and "irritating" character as Mame Dennis. Usually faithful to his honorable custom of not explaining to solicitous producers why a particular story did not interest him, Herbert made an exception in this case.

He wrote to Brisson: "I've never considered myself particularly squeamish, and I have no objections to profanity or obscenity, as such, when they are properly in context or appropriate to the background [of a story]; but I do gag at obscenity when it is put into the mouths of children, and I loathe it when used by the author merely to obtain what he believes to be a 'hilarious' result.

"These, however, are merely details," he continued. "My main quarrel is with the book itself, or, more accurately, with the character of Auntie Mame. Possibly I am so prejudiced that my judgment has been completely warped, but, at the moment, Freddie, I'll be damned if I can find one single, solitary redeeming quality in this character – or caricature – drawn by the author. Even a caricature can be affectionately or nostalgically drawn; Auntie

Mame has been so savagely and stupidly limned, so maliciously and obscenely distorted that she at no time even remotely resembles a human being. As such I find it impossible to imagine that anyone could conceivably find anything sympathetic about her – a prerequisite, I submit, that is mandatory for the protagonist in any literary form, whether it be a novel, a drama, a comedy or a musical.

"Auntie Mame, as depicted by the author, is idiotic and vulgar beyond words, shallow beyond belief, stupid beyond credulity. She is vain, frivolous, extravagant, profane, immoral, rude, ignorant, insincere and platitudinous. Is there anything that can be said in her favor? Yes – I suppose her defense of Jews should be credited to her, though hardly to the author who has penned, in that connection, one of the stupidest and most inept scenes I ever read. Mr. Dennis has an excellent vocabulary, and it's a pity that nobody ever drew his attention to the word 'subtlety' and all its delightful implications.

"The one quality completely lacking in both the book and the character of Auntie Mame is the priceless quality of charm. I have searched carefully for one charming thing that she does, says or even thinks, and I can't find one. And I think the same applies to every character in the novel, bar none.

"Don't misunderstand me," he added. "I'm aware of the fact that the author never intended us to take him seriously in his excursions into fancy. But a satire – if such it be – can even degenerate into burlesque and yet retain a few traces of wit and charm, dignity and decency. But not this book. In his grim resolve to make it 'screamingly funny' – determination so clear that one sees, on every page, a mental image of the author sweating at his typewriter – Mr. Dennis has, in my opinion, successfully alienated and nauseated every sensitive reader, every reader with a vestige of good taste, good will and good sense.

"A few weeks ago in New York, I saw the current smash comedy hit, 'No Time For Sergeants.' It's on a par with *Auntie Mame*.

I winced and writhed throughout the performance, while all around me delighted patrons howled with laughter.

"It's not inconceivable that these same people would howl with laughter if *Auntie Mame* should be done on the stage but I shudder to think of it. I know it's a best seller as a novel – and I shudder to think of that."

In closing his tirade to Brisson, Herbert cautioned, "Freddie, I have only one piece of advice to offer: if you decide to go ahead with it, for God's sake, throw every vestige of this offensive book out the window, and start from scratch."

Brisson was undoubtedly dismayed by Herbert's vitriolic reaction, but continued to pursue the project, intuitively trusting that any list of Mame's shortcomings could be balanced with an equally long list of her attributes, regardless of what F. Hugh Herbert believed.

As Rosalind Russell pointed out two years later, in a 1957 review for the Pocketbook edition of *Auntie Mame*: "In Mame's life there is little that is sacred. Here we come close to the secret of her charm. She is what every woman fondly hopes she is: an emotional realist. No matter what social conventions she outrages, she ends by making us feel that society's rules are more than a little silly. Like all great characters in comic literature, she has declared open war on sham and pretense. She has a needle to prick every stuffed shirt and lay bare the hypocrisies of the right and the snobbish, the privileged and the prejudiced of this world."

*

As time without a script went on, the Broadway death-wishers prophesied that *Auntie Mame* was a fascinating story but impossible to translate to the stage and that further script attempts would prove futile.

Jerome Lawrence, co-playwright with Robert E. Lee of some of the most successful Broadway shows of the past 40-years (most notably at that time "Inherit the Wind") recalls how he and Lee ultimately became the authors of the play: "'Auntie Mame' was a best-seller when I was in New York in December 1955. I was staying with a friend who had picked up a copy of the book and he was up all night reading it, screaming with laughter as I was trying to sleep in the guest room. When I got up the next morning, I said, 'If it's that funny, *I've* got to read it."

Lawrence did read *Auntie Mame* that very day and was immediately struck by the wonderful theatricality and universal appeal of the character. Instinctively, Lawrence knew that *Auntie Mame* was a property worth investigating as the source for the next Lawrence and Lee collaboration.

Jerome Lawrence easily convinced his partner of the potential significance of *Auntie Mame* as a comedy play and immediately contacted the author's representative Annie Laurie Williams, about purchasing the theatrical rights to the book. Williams advised them that Robert Fryer and Lawrence Carr shared their theatrical foresight and had already secured the dramatization rights, adding that they had unsuccessfully assigned Sumner Locke Elliott and then Patrick Dennis to the formidable task of adapting the property for the stage.

Williams concluded the conversation by promising that she would gladly approach the producers about Lawrence and Lee taking over the task.

At that time, Lawrence and Lee's now-classic "Inherit the Wind" was playing to standing-room-only eight performances a week at the National Theatre (re-opened in 1959 as The Billy Rose Theatre, and now the Nederlander), and Williams encouraged Fryer and Carr to attend a performance of the play as an introduction to the work of the two playwrights.

Playwright Jerome Lawrence (Author's collection)

The playwriting team of Jerome Lawrence (left) and Robertr E. Lee (right).
(Photo courtesey of Mrs. Robert E. Lee)

Fryer and Carr were as impressed with *Inherit the Wind* as the New York critics, especially with the unexpected wit in the dialogue. By the very next morning they decided to give Lawrence & Lee the assignment to write *Auntie Mame* with the strict proviso that a script had to be in their hands by March 15, 1956.

It had been more than a year since Fryer and Carr first approached Rosalind Russell with the idea of starring in a stage adaptation of *Auntie Mame*. She had spent eight months being indecisive about doing the play. Two important writers had already bitten the dust on the project and two more were now embarking on the task to come up with an acceptable script by the Ides of March.

On February 3, 1956, it was officially announced that Rosalind Russell had signed her Actors Equity contract to play Auntie Mame and within days it was speculated that Broadway star Orson Bean – who was currently starring in *Will Success Spoil Rock Hunter?* – would be the male lead.

With contracts signed by Rosalind Russell, Morton DaCosta and Jerome Lawrence and Robert E. Lee, the producers were confident that they could open their play on Broadway in about eight months.

"The same excitement that attended the birth of *Wonderful Town* is starting up again," Fryer enthused in a note to Russell. "And may I say, it's a wonderful feeling!"

CHAPTER THREE

The Making of a Hit Play

THE RUGGED and picturesque hills of Malibu, California, with their spectacular panoramic views of the Pacific Ocean allowing an occasional glimpse – on a clear, smogless day – of Santa Catalina Island, is not a typical image that comes to mind when one thinks of where hit Broadway plays are written. However, this is where Jerome Lawrence built his dream house, and where he and partner Robert E. Lee sequestered themselves to write *Auntie Mame*.

In retrospect, the hurdles that loomed before the playwrights appeared almost insurmountable. Already, two noted writers had failed to deliver an acceptable script, and though Lawrence and Lee were indeed prepared to tackle the creative challenge, the four-month deadline seemed unrealistic.

In addition, their libretto for *Shangri-La*, (a musical based on the classic James Hilton novel *Lost Horizon*), was simultaneously being produced by Fryer and Carr and eventually opened on Broadway, June 13, 1956. As the two authors took on the formidable task of writing *Auntie Mame*, they were also *rewriting Shangri-La*.

The origin of the playwriting team known as Lawrence and Lee began almost 15 years earlier. Though they both grew up in Ohio (a scant 30 miles apart), the two did not meet until 1942 when both were forging careers in New York, writing for radio programs.

Together, their accomplishments, writing first for radio and then theatre, have made them one of the most important literary teams in theatre history – and arguably the longest collaborators in the English language – ever to merge their talents. The harvest of their collaborative efforts include *Look, Ma, I'm Dancin'!* (1948), *Inherit the Wind* (1955), *Only in America* (1959), *The Gang's All Here* (1959), *Diamond Orchid* (1965), *Mame* (1966), *Dear World* (1969), *The Night Thoreau Spent in Jail* (1971), *Jabberwock* (1972), *First Monday in October* (1978) and *Whisper in the Mind* (1990).

It was now early 1956. The two writers fortified themselves by re-reading the *Auntie Mame* novel many times, absorbing the characters and the story, and discussing how to approach the tremendous task at hand.

"The first scene at the cocktail party is going to be difficult," they agreed. "As we all know there is nothing harder or duller to write or stage than a cocktail party, especially with characters that may not interest the average audience too much. At times Mame acts like a real idiot and not a real person. We've often said that everyone has an Auntie Mame in their family or knows of an Auntie Mame, but even at that she must be a more realistic person than the one written in the book."

Getting the crucial Mame Dennis character down on paper was obviously the primary challenge, but the authors took equal care with the supporting members of the story. As they plotted their narration, Lawrence and Lee sketched the ancillary characters:

• *Young Patrick*: A completely natural, inquisitive, unprecocious child who progresses from age 10 to 14 years through the play.
• *Adult Patrick*: Attractive, easy-going, charming, good sense of humor and urbane. Starts at 19 years of age, ends at 31.
• *Vera Charles*: A scheming dame from Pittsburgh who has fought her way up the ladder to become one of our top "classic" actresses. When we meet Vera, her popularity in the theatre is just beginning to wane. Tall, blonde, statuesque, about 40. Best exaggerated "standard diction" which, when she is under duress, lapses into the most nasal aspects of Pittsburgh diction.

• *Beauregard*: Big, handsome, in his 40s. Plantation owner, thick Southern accent, but as real as his charm. Dynamic and chivalrous.
• *Mother Burnside*: An enormous harridan in her sixties. Unyielding Southern matriarch. She booms like a foghorn and is just as flatulent. She burps her way through life.
• *Sally Cato MacDougal*: A peaches and cream Southern belle in her 30s. Beautiful and under the treacle, terrible.
• *Gloria Upson*: A pretty, stiff-lipped, frozen-faced empty-headed society girl. Early 20s.
• *Agnes Gooch*: Flat-heeled, secretary. First seen as completely unattractive girl who lives with her mother and knows nothing of the world. Mame transforms her into something of a dish.

*

By January 24, 1955, Rosalind Russell reported to her friend Annie Laurie Williams that she was very excited with the way the Lawrence and Lee script was progressing. "It seems that all is going well with [*Auntie*] *Mame* and I couldn't be happier," she wrote. "Bobby [Lee] and Jerry [Lawrence] are hard at it and from all reports the completed scenes have flavor, heart and fun. As you know, I was upset for fear they would not be able to devote their time to 'our project' but my latest carrier pigeon tells me that *Shangri-La* will be postponed if they can't get the right director, until after [*Auntie*] *Mame* hits the boards."

However, a director for *Shangri-la* was chosen (Albert Marre), and the show, starring Dennis King, Alice Ghostley, Jack Cassidy, Martyn Green and Shirley Yamaguchi went into production. But, as John McClain in the *New York Journal-American* wrote, "*Shangri-la* has had something less than a Utopian history: Several important members of the cast left after the opening in Boston, the director was replaced, and the authors finally stopped the proceedings and did almost an entire re-write."

"I've been trying to follow *Shangri-la* via the New York and local trade papers, plus various people who phone from New York," Russell again wrote to Williams. "It seems to be in serious trouble and proves once again that good old Freddie [husband, Brisson] should be around for *Auntie Mame*. However, that is in the past and I know he would not consider it now."

In a questionable turn of events, a rift developed between Fryer, Carr and Brisson, the facts of which remain undisclosed: Carr died in 1969, Brisson passed away in 1984, and Mr. Fryer does not recall that Brisson was ever involved at any time. Though written documents reveal otherwise, the consequence remains the same: Brisson resigned completely and forever from any formal participation in *Auntie Mame*.

With all the chaos going on, director DaCosta plowed away on production plans and schedules for *Auntie Mame*, creating casting charts and hiring the technical people for the show.

"I'm hoping that DaCosta is a firm and steady man," Russell skeptically wrote to Annie Laurie. "He will have to be," she stressed. "I know Fryer and Carr well and their weaknesses. As you know, I begged them not to attempt *Shangri-La* this season but to concentrate on an already proven property, our *Auntie Mame*."

Alas, *Shangri-La*, with book and lyrics by Jerome Lawrence and Robert E. Lee and *Lost Horizon* novelist James Hilton, opened on Broadway, but the notices for the musical were too tepid to draw audiences sufficient enough to stay open at the Winter Garden Theatre. The show closed after only 21 performances. Lawrence and Lee were finally free to devote their full concentration to *Auntie Mame*.

*

It was determined from early on that the costumes and sets for *Auntie Mame* would be high-style glamour. This was to be a musical-sized show with the look and feel of a major musical production – without the music.

For the sets and costumes, DaCosta met simultaneously with acclaimed designers Cecil Beaton and Oliver Smith. Though both were equally respected as set designers, Beaton was DaCosta's first choice to create both the stage sets and clothes. Although Beaton had other obligations and could not be in New York for some time, he reluctantly agreed to participate in the new production of *Auntie Mame*.

DaCosta, however, sensed the designer's lack of enthusiasm for the project and feared that he might be difficult to retain on the project. As DaCosta feared, even after Beaton had given a verbal agreement, he soon recanted. "Well, my hunch was right," DaCosta reported to Rosalind Russell, "Beaton has backed out. He's afraid of doing a multi-scene show like [*Auntie*] *Mame* – doesn't feel he's up to it. He says he's exhausted and wants to vacation for a month. I asked if he would at least do the costumes and he refused, with regrets, but adamantly."

Instead, DaCosta hired Oliver Smith, who immediately appeared to be very enthusiastic about the project. "Maybe it's for the best as I can work with Smith at once and in person," DaCosta reasoned in a letter to Russell.

*

Writing and molding the project had been a day and night process for the playwrights, and finally, four months after their initial assignment, Lawrence and Lee tucked the first draft of the play into an envelope and sent the manuscript via Special Delivery to DaCosta. Their cover note advised, "This script was typed by a very sweet Hindustani lady who learned stenography from Auntie Mame, so forgive typos…" DaCosta read the complete script and sent a copy to Rosalind Russell for her comments.

Changes are inevitable with any literary project, though perhaps none more than a stage script; encompassing seemingly endless re-writes, honing the dialogue and sharpening the stage direction. Once the script's first draft had been submitted to DaCosta, the task of editing began.

During the weekend of July 20-21, Rosalind Russell and Robert E. Lee met at her home in Beverly Hills to further discuss the play and to allow Russell to comment on each scene. After the intense two-day summit, pouring over the pages of the first draft with their star, the playwrights resumed editing their manuscript with notes from the Russell/Lee meeting.

"Beginning with Act I, Scene 2," they asked themselves, "could the action of the cocktail party which opens the play actually be over and only a handful of people left in [Auntie Mame's] drawing room? Perhaps we could see one or two people exiting when little Patrick and Norah arrive. Two or three people exiting and being slightly intoxicated and practically knocking Norah and Pat over would be very upsetting to Norah and would establish her as being very annoyed with this madhouse she is about to enter. We must be sure that Norah does not accept the insane life at Beekman Place too quickly. She should look on the houseboy Ito as a heathen; and, as a good Catholic, she is appalled at all the drinking and only gradually during the course of the play does she realize how good Mame really is."

This kind of intense analyzing re-shaped the mechanics of the play. The story and basic structure were unquestionably already there but during the next several months, until the first rehearsal at the Broadhurst Theatre, the playwrights would continue interpreting characters and adjusting dialogue until the whole play functioned smoothly as a single unit and no aspect caused the slightest bit of friction.

It was less than a month before rehearsals were to begin in New York, and during the next few weeks, the playwrights tightened their script, meticulously brushing up the subtlest reference such as the price of a suit that Mame owned, or how Young Patrick was to mix a martini for his trustee, Mr. Babcock the banker: "Not too expert at mixing," they noted. "Swills Vermouth, then pours it out. Doing it by rote, cautious, more endearing."

Act One introduced Mame, Patrick, Norah and the manipu- lative banker, Babcock, and took the action of the play from the height of the Jazz Age to the depths of the Great Depression. Mame goes from being a rich dilettante, to a poor working girl employed in various capacities including a telephone switch- board operator, sales clerk and a bit player in a stage production with her best friend Vera Charles. She is fired successively from each of these positions.

Referring to the scene where Mame has been given two small lines of dialogue in Vera's play, *Midsummer Madness*, Russell was adamant; "As far as Scene 8, it should be positively out," she demanded. "It has always been proven dull on the stage or screen to do a play-within-a-play, especially with phony charac- ters and phony dialogue and this doesn't prove anything at all!"

For all of Russell's theatrical integrity, there were times when her intuition just didn't pay off. The skillful way in which Lawrence and Lee wrote the scene would prove to be one of the most hilarious in the show.

Another of those occasions occurred during rehearsals and out-of-town tryouts in what was affectionately known as "The Ping Pong Scene." The action is the last party sequence in the play and Auntie Mame has invited her closest, albeit campy and eccentric friends, to meet Patrick's fiancée Gloria Upson and her anti-Semitic parents, Claude and Doris. Gloria has the guests nervously listening to her silly tragedy about having to call off a ping pong game at her snobby country club because she stepped on the ping pong ball and "just squashed it to nothing! It was ghastly. It was just ghastly!"

"And I stepped on the Ping-Pong ball!" Gloria Upson (Joyce Lear, center) recounts a moronic tragedy of losing a Ping-Pong game at her snobby country club as a captive audience listens with polite contempt, including (left to right) Ralph Devine (Grant Sullivan), M. Lindsay Woolsey (John O'Hare), Mame Dennis (Rosalind Russell) and Vera Charles (Polly Rowles), in the original 1956 Broadway production of *Auntie Mame*. (Courtesy of James Monks)

As Jerome Lawrence tells it, "All during rehearsal, both Tec DaCosta and Roz claimed that the scene wasn't funny and that no one would laugh. They both wanted the scene cut. We said, 'Listen, play it one night in Wilmington, that's all we ask! If it doesn't get laughs, we'll be the first to agree to remove it.' The night of the opening in Wilmington, Bob [Lee] and I were in the stage wings, watching as airhead Gloria began her sniveling lament about the idiotic catastrophe at the club. The audience laughed so hysterically that it stopped the show cold. Roz ran off stage, grabbed us, and whispered, 'Don't you dare cut ping pong!'

"To be frank, we weren't really sure whether it would work either, but we fell on the floor laughing while we were writing it. We had to give it a chance."

*

As the August 16th date for Russell to leave Los Angeles for rehearsals in New York loomed closer, she was understandably nervous and yet restless to get started with the play. According to her husband Frederick's personal diary, Rosalind was "a bundle of nerves" and understandably suffered from insomnia prior to her departure. It was a time of great anticipation, excitement and trepidation for the star. With her film career on the wane, and since her last stage venture had been such a great triumph (she won the 1953 Tony Award for best actress in a musical for *Wonderful Town*), she was concerned about maintaining her star status.

Russell spent the entire afternoon of August 11th being fitted by designer Travis Banton in Beverly Hills for her *Auntie Mame* stage costumes. Her beautiful stage wardrobe was among the more expensive aspects of the costly production and using the talents of Mr. Banton was a testimony to Russell's allegiance to friends. In addition to her legendary acting and business skills,

Rosalind Russell (James Monks collection)

Russell was equally regarded as a very loyal and giving human being. When it came time to select a designer for her stage wardrobe she insisted that Travis Banton be hired.

That was a particularly touching gesture for although Banton had once been a very successful and respected motion picture costume designer, by the time the *Auntie Mame* project materialized, his fame had eclipsed to near extinction. He had fallen on hard times and was considered by many to be all but washed up in the business. Robert Fryer recalls that Russell insisted on using Banton. "It's unfair that he has been abandoned. I found Jean Louis and Jimmy Galanos and I tell you that this man could make a big comeback with *Auntie Mame*," Fryer remembers the star exclaiming.

"She was very insistent that he be signed as her designer," Fryer recalls. "After that, he had his own line of clothes and became very successful again. She was a very loyal friend."

"I designed the fashions for Rosalind Russell in *Auntie Mame* with a tongue-in-cheek exaggeration," explained Banton in a magazine article, "because fashions amuse Auntie Mame. The play covers a period of about twenty years from the late-1920s on, but I didn't caricature the fashions of the times because Mame is no caricature. She's an eccentric, and like all true eccentrics, she has a contempt for the banal."

Banton began his career in the theatre creating costumes for the *Ziegfeld Follies* and other stage musicals, before going to Hollywood. He had frequently created designs for Russell to wear in her movies over the years and he adored working with her. "I have found her one of the most intelligent women I've ever known," he said. "Like Auntie Mame, she knows what she wants and what's right for her to wear. It should surprise no one that Rosalind Russell is playing Auntie Mame. The two are so much alike that Roz told me she was plain scared. She said,

'Everybody thinks I'm so right for the part they'll expect miracles that can't possibly happen.'"

On the 16th of August, a nervous Russell boarded the train in Pasadena, California, with her personal maid, Blanche Williams, and settled in for the journey to Manhattan, via Chicago. When she arrived at New York's Grand Central Station aboard the Twentieth Century Limited, on Saturday, August 18, she was met by her chauffeur in a new Fleetwood 60 and taken to the Pierre Hotel on Fifth Avenue at 61st Street where she had rented a $750 a month suite for the run-of-the-play.

Frugal star that she was, it was arranged that the suite would be sublet (with the exception of one room to be used for Russell's storage) during her vacation or out-of-town absences from the play. As a result, the apartment would not cost her anything while she was not in residence.

Monday, August 20th was a drizzling, cheerless day all up and down the Eastern seaboard. But when Rosalind arrived at the Broadhurst Theatre, at precisely 10:00 a.m., she was met with radiant smiles by director Morton DaCosta and stage manager Robert Linden, both of whom were fervently trying to complete the play's casting. Though DaCosta had been working on this aspect of the play since July, there were still several key roles that did not have players or suitable actors assigned to them. One of those was the pivotal role of Agnes Gooch, the mousy secretary who is transformed by Mame's prodding into a would-be *femme fatale*.

Peggy Cass – who went on to win a best supporting actress Tony Award for the role – remembers, "I was in Dallas doing another show when my agent, Gus Schirmer, called me and said I had to come to New York to read for *Auntie Mame*. I was hell-bent to go to California to be in the movies, but he wanted me to read for the part of the Irish maid, Norah Muldoon. I came to New York, arrived at the theatre and went onto the stage of the Broadhurst. I read for the maid and they just said, 'Thank you...'

"As I was about to leave, there was a buzz from the audience and Rosalind said, 'Let her read for the understudy of Agnes Gooch.'

"Gus took me down to the basement of the Broadhurst and I told him, 'I don't want to read for this part! I want to play the maid! This part's nothing! It doesn't have any lines!'

"He said, 'It's a brilliant part, now you read it."

Cass studied the part with Schirmer, and when everybody else had read for the day, stage manager Robert Linden approached her and said, "Miss Russell would like you to read now."

Cass expected to read with Linden, as everybody else had. Much to her surprise, however, Rosalind Russell came onto the stage to read Act II, Scene 6 in which Auntie Mame transforms Gooch from a mousy secretary into an attractive, sophisticated society woman. In this Pygmalion-like scene, Mame insists that Agnes respond to her direction. Pointing to Gooch's strange-looking shoes, she implores, "What do you call those things?"

"Orthopedic oxfords," Agnes shrieks.

"Kick 'em off!" Mame demands.

Cass kicked so high that her shoes flew into the wings. Russell exclaimed, "That's my Gooch!"

"So I got the part," Cass fondly recalls. "I always felt a little guilty because another actress already had been told that she had it. But after I read, they didn't sign her contract. I also understudied five other parts – all for $125 a week!"

The salaries, apart from Russell's, were absolutely rock bottom, Equity minimum. There's an old saying in the theatre: "Actors are either praying to get into a hit or to get out of one," and *Auntie Mame* appeared to be headed for a long run, so the minimum pay was balanced by the prospect of a steady weekly paycheck.

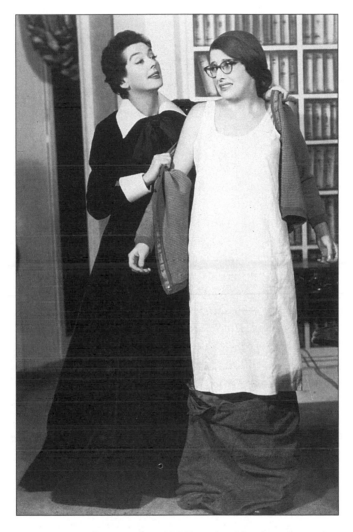

Peggy Cass (right) won the 1956 Tony Award as best supporting actress for her role as the mousy secretary Agnes Gooch, who is transformed by Auntie Mame's (Rosalind Russell) affirmative "Life is a banquet" philosophy. (Courtesy of James Monks)

Dorothy Blackburn, one of the most respected Broadway character actresses of the day, remembers that when she auditioned for the part of Mrs. Upson she was initially horrified by the prejudice of the character.

"I had a great deal of experience on Broadway," she modestly admits, "and they called me in to read for the part of Doris Upson. When I arrived at the theatre, for some reason they said the director wanted me to read for Norah, the maid. I read for that part, and some time passed before I was called in again for a second reading. I thought I was coming back to read for Norah, but when I arrived at the Broadhurst Theatre stage door I was handed some lines for Doris Upson. When I read the scene I was so shocked, I didn't know what in the world I would do.

"Doris Upson made very slighting remarks about nationality and religion. I knew I could not go out on any stage and speak that way about any group of people. What in the world was I going to do?

"All of a sudden I remembered a woman I had known when I was living in the suburbs. Though she was really a lovely person, she didn't have a thought in her head that wasn't her husband's. I decided, if I make Doris a person without any brains, nobody could take any offense from what she says. So that's how I created the Doris character, pretty much on the spur of the moment."

Blackburn's career in the theatre began when she danced on the same program with Nijinski, at the Metropolitan Opera in New York. Over the ensuing years, Blackburn was a favorite of Broadway audiences, performing with more 20 of the most celebrated leading players of her day including Ethel Barrymore, Wallace Ettinger, Leo Carroll, Jane Powell, Edward Everett Horton, Helen Hayes, Jimmy Stewart, Billie Burke, Douglas Fairbanks, Jr., Ruth Gordon and Leslie Howard.

In addition to the theatre, Blackburn appeared on innumerable television programs including such early live-broadcast series as *Robert Montgomery Presents* where she played a different role every Monday night.

Casting for the other roles continued throughout the week, during which time the director, producers, playwrights and Miss Russell sat through hundreds of auditions. Selecting the juvenile lead was perhaps one of the most tricky challenges in the arduous process of assigning an actor to each part.

To the successful candidate for the role of young Patrick Dennis, several important prerequisites were attached; not the least of which was a rapport with the star. In addition to portraying an innocent yet precocious child, it was essential that the actor express a synergy with Russell. Intelligence, teamwork, harmony, unity – those unique attributes were finally found in young Jan Handzlik, whose mother answered an ad in the paper: "Wanted – A boy with an Ivy League look, good stage presence and must be unspoiled."

Jan Handzlik starred as young Patrick Dennis to Rosalind Russell's Auntie Mame. (Courtesy of James Monks)

Now a prominent attorney in Los Angeles, specializing in white collar criminal defense, Handzlik has clear and fond memories of his auspicious career as a young actor.

"I started in summer stock when I was 7-years old, appearing in plays and musicals," he says. "Though my mom was not a stage mother, she heard about the auditions for young Patrick and took me into New York to try out at the Broadhurst Theatre. I went to the auditions along with about five hundred other kids, and after reading for the part, I was chosen.

"Miss Russell was very caring, very concerned with me as a person," Handzlik says. "With respect to my scenes, she worked very hard with me, to develop a nice even cadence."

*

On Monday, August 27, the entire cast (minus Jimmy Kirkwood who had been cast as the Mature Patrick) gathered on stage at the Broadhurst Theatre for the first day of rehearsal. Jimmy Kirkwood, who would go on to become a successful author and playwright (*P.S. Your Cat Is Dead*, *A Chorus Line*), was originally cast as the Mature Patrick Dennis but was abruptly terminated, almost as soon as rehearsals began.

Several versions of why he was replaced still abound in conversations about the play. "He had a terrible run-in with Miss Russell from the beginning," says one cast member. "Rosalind was downright nasty to him. I don't know why and he never knew why. She could be nasty to a lot of juveniles if they didn't suit her, and after all, they were playing her nephew. She wanted someone she was simpatico with. We had an array of people playing that role."

Another cast member reveals, "Every now and then somebody would disappear. One person was let out because he came in and was slightly drunk one night – not in the performance, but in a rehearsal. In the beginning we were all worried. But after the sixth day of rehearsal everybody relaxed because for the first five days they can fire you without pay."

Still another cast member recalls that Kirkwood merely had a time conflict because of another job and wasn't available to start rehearsals for three or four days. "He was doing a soap opera. I don't know who that didn't suit, but it didn't suit someone very much and they canned him." Kirkwood was indeed engaged for a daily live broadcast from New York in the popular 15-minute soap opera *Valiant Lady*, in which he played the role of Mickey Emerson until August 16, 1957.

The official press announcement on September 5, 1956 simply read, "Final script revisions of *Auntie Mame* altered the conception of the character of the Adult Patrick, with the result that Jimmy Kirkwood who was first engaged for the role, has been replaced by Robert Higgins." This didn't exactly fool anybody in the theatre, but at least it was a dignified way to announce the termination.

The principals now included Beulah Garrick as nursemaid Norah; Jan Handzlik as Young Patrick; Yuki Shimoda as Ito, the giggling Japanese houseboy; Polly Rowles as the sodden actress Vera Charles; Peggy Cass as Gooch; James Monks as Mame's Irish lover Brian O'Bannion; Robert Smith as Beauregard Jackson Pickett Burnside; Robert Higgins (as the Mature Patrick); and Dorothy Blackburn as Mrs. Upson. "From that point on," said director DaCosta, "we all became very communal."

Almost from the beginning of Rosalind Russell's participation in the play, there was talk that she was really responsible for writing the script for *Auntie Mame*. Legend has Russell locking herself in her hotel room one night, emerging the next morning with the first act entirely re-written. In her autobiography,

Russell indeed suggested that she and director Tec DaCosta re-wrote the Lawrence and Lee play themselves.

But DaCosta refutes this: "When Roz's book came out they asked me to give it a blurb. I said, 'I would love to because I adored Roz, but I cannot endorse all of the fantasy in it.' There were a lot of, shall we say, *liberties* taken in that book. She even said that I was her choice for director after catching my work on *No Time For Sergeants*. Well, that's a lot of crap."

In a letter from Greer Garson to co-playwright Robert E. Lee, sometime after she replaced Russell as Auntie Mame on Broadway, she alluded to the same story about Roz claiming to have written the script. "With Jerry's [Lawrence] approval and encouragement," she wrote, "I added a new tack to the telephone switchboard scene ... I thought this would amuse you as you must both be inured by now to the bold claims of actresses who inform the world that they have written your play! I notice that, having tried to steal your thunder, a certain lady is now expressing resentment that Patrick Dennis wrote the original book, as she herself had the whole thing in mind and in notes and was on the point of publishing it! How far can an over-worked imagination go, or is it a possessive mania that arises from a successful appearance in a certain character and mucho publicity?"

James Monks, who played the Irish poet/lothario Brian O'Bannion, remembers, "Rosalind knew what fit her as an actress. I don't know whose idea it was, but in my big scene with her my character was made pure as the driven snow, which of course I wasn't. Somewhere between the book version and the play, the character was emasculated."

Russell's good friend Cris Alexander, who played four small parts in the show, understudied the Mature Patrick Dennis, and who knew Russell perhaps better than anyone in the production,

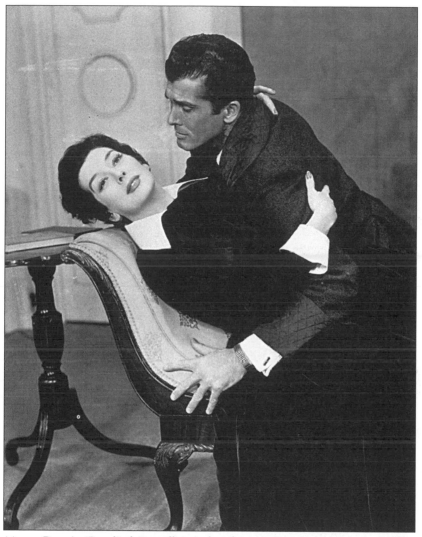

Mame Dennis (Rosalind Russell) can barely resist being swept away by the charms of handsome lothario Brian O'Bannion (James Monks) in the 1956 Broadway production of *Auntie Mame*. (Courtesy of James Monks)

says, "It was fascinating to see it all begin to add up. It was fascinating to me because I was crazy about the book – who wasn't? Rosalind had a great deal to do with it being a success. But she didn't sit down and re-write the script, she didn't sit down and cross out a line and write another. She may have had something to do with that wonderful telephone-operator sketch."

"Not *one* syllable!" Lawrence & Lee affirm.

*

Rehearsals for *Auntie Mame* began at 10:00 a.m. sharp on Monday, August 27 at the Broadhurst Theatre.

The Broadhurst had been good luck for Fryer & Carr's production of *The Desk Set* the previous season, and the producers contracted with the Shubert Organization for use of their theatre again.

"The Broadhurst has always been a favorite of mine," recalls Jerome Lawrence. "When I was in college, I used to hitchhike to New York, and I remember going there to see Helen Hayes in *Victoria Regina*. I know the exact seat I sat in, it was the second row of the mezzanine, two seats from the left-hand side. During rehearsals of *Auntie Mame*, I used to go up there and sit in the same seat and watch the stage."

"Rehearsals were very much like rehearsals for any show," remembers Cris Alexander who also became one of novelist Patrick Dennis' best friends. It was also the first time the cast met the novel's author.

"He (Dennis) was at the height of his dandyism," recalls Alexander of his eminent friend. "He wore a mustache and beautifully trimmed beard. Directly after lunch during the first read-through of the script, in came this really eccentric sight with the most affected pronunciation. He came into the theatre holding his umbrella, and addressed Miss Russell and the cast. He appeared so pompous that when he left everybody just looked at each other. We were absolutely speechless.

"I had never seen anybody like him. I didn't realize at the time that he was just playing the part of the author. But when he came on the road with us everything fell into place. He was *playing* a part. He was just absolutely witty, and I dare say that first speech he gave to us was witty – except that nobody was primed for it. We thought he was dead serious. He liked to make an impression for the sake of making an impression."

It was evident during the first couple of weeks of rehearsal that Tec DaCosta and Rosalind felt nervous about the show. It was a big cast and everybody was very serious. There was not much playtime or laughter or reaction and few of the actors related personally to each other. Everybody did what was required of them and that was it.

Polly Rowles, who portrayed the second-banana Vera Charles, remembers rehearsals well. "We all got along fine on stage, but the relationship ended at the stage door. I don't mean that we weren't friendly. We just didn't share our lives at all.

"But it was fun playing with Rosalind," she continues. "She was extremely supportive and loved working in this. She really sparkled. She was very generous, she liked others to get laughs too. She wasn't one of those awful creatures that feels that everything has to be directed toward her."

Robert Smith, who played the love interest Beauregard, recalls that one night after rehearsal he and Rowles got together for drinks and to discuss their respective characters. Polly complained, "I'm very upset with my part, I can't seem to get a hold of it. I don't know what's wrong."

Smith was an astute observer. "Do you want me to tell you what you're doing wrong?" he asked. "You're playing it as though Roz is the star and you're a featured player. In the play *you* are the star and Roz is just a walk-on. You're playing up to her and you should be playing down to her. You should dominate all your scenes!"

Heeding this advice, Rowles was brilliant in the part and she walked away with excellent notices from every critic.

Beauregard Jackson Pickett Burnside (Robert Smith) is Mame's (Rosalind Russell) southern knight in shining armor, in the 1956 Broadway production of *Auntie Mame*. (Courtesy of James Monks)

Smith was equally alert when it came to his own performance. He remembers that the laughs for his marriage-proposal scene to Mame started to disappear during the out-of-town performances. "I'm down on my knees in my hunting outfit and I'm saying, 'could you...would you...' in preparation for a proposal of marriage to Mame. All of a sudden I'm interrupted by the hunting bugle.

"At first I would get enormous applause. But my laughs started to disappear.

"Usually, when the star can cut your laughs, they're happy. But Roz called me into her dressing room one night and said, 'Bob, you're losing your laughs.' I said, 'I know I am and I watch myself to see if I'm doing anything different but my performance hasn't changed a bit.'

"She said, 'You're not doing anything different; you play it exactly the same way every night with the same energy. *I'm* doing something different. I'm moving too fast. Tonight I'll be like a stone monument.'

"That night the laughs came in like gangbusters. Backstage she said, 'I knew it!' That's a wonderful tribute to a leading lady."

Peggy Cass remembers, "Rosalind never once tried to tone me down. She was always trying to build me up. She said that by the time I came on – which was the beginning of the second act – the audience had seen so much of her, she had carried so much of the show, that they were damn glad to see me. They say how some stars cut you down and reduce your part if you get too much attention. I never had that experience with Roz. She was absolutely out for the good of the play."

A few days into the rehearsal, DaCosta made a strange but funny request, an announcement that created enormous laughter among the cast. "Is there anybody here who can belch at will?" he asked with a grin. The bright and sophisticated Cris

Alexander remembered that as a child he had belched a great deal, as youngsters are wont to do. However, there hadn't been much call for that sort of immature antic since he was about fourteen. "But, I stood up and said. I can do that!"

"Oh, show us, Cris!" Russell implored with a big smile. "So I took a large intake of breath," Alexander recalls, – "and brought it back up. It was so funny that it just knocked her and everyone else over! "So, I had another job in the show," he says. "Every night I stood with a megaphone behind a big window on the set of the Peckerwood mansion set, and on cue I belched for the Mother Burnside character.

"Every night we had from six to ten stagehands cheering me on for the belch. In between set changes and between matinees, those same stagehands were in a room directly above the stage showing dirty movies. When I told Rosalind, I thought she'd never stop laughing. She said, 'I don't have enough time off between changes to go up and watch them!'"

Time was certainly something that Russell lacked between costume changes. To expedite matters and because she was temporarily blinded after each quick blackout, the management at the Broadhurst mercifully employed six assistant stage managers who, by turns, rushed on stage after each scene, to pilot the star to her dressing spot. Her more elaborate costume changes required up to six assistants – and one flashlight bearer. One evening, just before the end of the first act, she ran full force into an equally hurried stagehand. The collision buckled the stars legs, brought tears to her eyes and nearly knocked her unconscious. During intermission she was attended to by the house physician but she refused medication for fear it would dull her timing.

*

On September 18, the cast left New York for Delaware. After a series of successful run-throughs of the play, the cast left feeling as though the show was in pretty good shape. In Wilmington, the production crew dressed the stage and the cast continued rehearsing, trusting that after the first performance before a live audience, there undoubtedly would be further changes. When the curtain came down after the first preview on September 22, Russell was hoarse from rehearsing all day, but fairly happy with the audience's reaction. All the laughs were in the rights places and *Auntie Mame* had heart and soul. Back in her hotel suite that night, she gathered Fryer and Carr, Lawrence and Lee and Cris Alexander to discuss the show and some changes she wanted before the official September 24 opening.

"But we did very little re-writing out of town, we just made a few cuts," recalls Jerome Lawrence. We cut one scene where Mame was a fashion model and some fat old man kept pinching her behind."

This was during the series of vignettes after Mame loses her fortune and is forced to go to work. "Mame must be deadly serious about each job, and every time she is fired, she must be broken by it," Russell insisted.

"Then we'd better have a spare 'job' ready for Mame, in case the modeling doesn't quite work," Lawrence and Lee had intuitively agreed before they left New York.

"One other thing we changed out of town," Lawrence says, "occurred at the very end of the play. We had a fairly longer scene with the Pegeen Ryan (Mame's private secretary) and the Adult Patrick characters at the end of the second act in order for Roz to change into a sari. Out-of-town we decided that we mustn't let Roz off stage. So we wrote a telegram wire for her to read while changing out of the audience's view. But she was never really off stage because you hear her voice. We had previously written the scene with Pegeen and Patrick talking, but we missed having Roz present."

*

Opening night in Wilmington was an actor's dream-come-true. The critics were delighted and the audience wildly enthusiastic.

The following morning, Philip F. Crosland of the *Delaware Journal* said, "*Auntie Mame* had her formal introduction to Wilmington last night at the Playhouse and I wonder if the town will ever be the same. Auntie Mame is a sort of Perle Mesta, Elsa Maxwell, Gisele MacKenzie and Little Miss Marker all rolled into one. If Miss Russell is to be remembered for one stage play we wager it will be this one."

Betty Burroughs of the *Wilmington Morning News* was equally enthusiastic about every aspect of the production. "Another standout performance is turned in by Susan Steel in the unsavory role of Mother Burnside," the critic wrote.

However, despite her excellent notices, Steel became another casualty of the tight ship that Russell presided over. She was described by fellow-actor Cris Alexander as "one of the bawdiest, funniest, dearest old fat ladies that ever lived and she was a brilliant performer."

"When she came into the play she was positively magnificent," remembers Robert Smith. "However one night in Philadelphia she had a little too much to drink and was unable to perform. She was immediately dismissed. That was the last of her."

Dorothy Blackburn remembers that, in addition to her own role as Mrs. Upson, she understudied other parts in the production including that of the corpulent Mrs. Burnside: "I understudied many times during my career on Broadway and was always horrified by the prospect of coming to the theatre and having the stage manager say, 'You're on tonight!'"

The night in Philadelphia when Miss Steel was unable to perform, Blackburn's nightmare came true. "I arrived at the theatre already made up for the Macy's department store scene [for another small part she played] wearing a red wig and big glasses so that nobody would recognize me when I came on later as Doris Upson. They yanked off the red wig and put on another wig and said, 'Susan Steel is out. You're going on as Mother Burnside!'"

A terrifying night such as that is one that could never be forgotten. The actress described the chaotic scene: "Director Tec DaCosta came down to the basement of the theatre where my dressing room was and we quickly began running lines. There was no time to think it over; it was time to go on stage. Since the curtain had already gone up, there was panic because we didn't know how we were going to get word to Rosalind that I was taking over as Mrs. Burnside. It was really like a circus.

"Finally, my scene started and Tec said he would be behind one of the pillars on the plantation set to prompt me. The scene began. I was up on the porch of the Peckerwood plantation for the fox hunt and everything was going fine. All of a sudden, my mind snapped back thirty-five years to when I was the leading woman in a play called *The Hottentot*, in Dayton, Ohio. The whole theatre and *Auntie Mame* melted away and there I was back in that play about a horse race.

"I finished the scene and there was thunderous applause at the end, but it was pointed out after the performance that the scene was that of a fox hunt *not* a horse race!"

After a successful weekend of *Auntie Mame* in Wilmington, Russell had exhausted her voice, but she was relatively happy with the way the production was shaping up. They moved on to the Forrest Theatre in Philadelphia for two weeks starting October 2.

"Where most writers have to stay up all night for rewrites with new shows, nothing had to be done in Philadelphia," says Jerome Lawrence. "Nothing, except a few cuts here and there.

Everything was so peaceful that we even took Roz to the movies on a couple of days when there weren't matinees."

The remarkably tranquil climate wasn't exactly great news for everybody however. The popular periodical *The Ladies Home Journal* had given author Patrick Dennis an assignment to cover the out-of-town rehearsal and performances of *Auntie Mame* for a story about the caustic backstage biting and bickering that often accompanies the pre-Broadway preparation for a stage show. They paid the author $3,500 to dish the dirt on the actors, and to blow the whistle on how temperamental the star was, and how everybody was literally at each others' throats. But Dennis found there was nothing on which to base such an exposé. The out-of-town rehearsals and performances were so pleasant and enjoyable that he couldn't come up with enough material to stoke a steamy paragraph, let along an entire article.

Director DaCosta remembers, "When we were in Wilmington, he called my hotel room in an absolute dither. He could be an absolute nut. He screamed, 'You're not having any trouble! I can't write the God-damned magazine piece!' He ultimately – and furiously – had to refund the magazine's money."

The out-of-town period with *Auntie Mame* was an especially pleasing time in the lives of both Rosalind Russell and her husband. Two of the musicals that Brisson had produced for Broadway were celebrating auspicious anniversaries: *The Pajama Game* was completing its 1,000th performance, while *Damn Yankees* had just played to its 600th audience. The Brissons were on top as far as the theatre world was concerned.

But soon Russell was less than enthusiastic about her own show *Auntie Mame*. It was a Friday, and she phoned her husband in California after the evening performance with a husky voice. She had a cold, and was tired and nervous and somewhat upset because the show had received a poor audience reaction that night.

*

Over the rutted road which a production travels toward Broadway success or failure, the critical notices for *Auntie Mame* during the out-of-town tryouts were unanimously effusive, in praise of both the production and its star. The reviews in each city en route to the "Great White Way" – Wilmington, Philadelphia and Washington, D.C. – proclaimed the show to be one of the most hilarious satires of the past quarter century; and by the end of the completely sold-out tryouts, odds were that "Auntie Mame" would be the biggest hit on Broadway during the 1956-57 season. The *Philadelphia Inquirer* prophesied, "If Miss Russell can survive the pace, she has the hit of her career on her hands."

But could she last? That was the question on the minds of even Russell's most optimistic friends. Indeed, *Auntie Mame* was the supreme achievement of Rosalind Russell's illustrious theatrical career and the star immediately became synonymous with the mythical Mame Dennis-Burnside. Every performer dreams of a signature role and, for Rosalind Russell, *Auntie Mame* became that singular portrayal for which she is most remembered – and beloved.

In 1956, one could hardly recall a non-musical with the critical and fiscal impact of *Auntie Mame*. Carrying a hefty price tag of $180,000 to mount the production, it was among the costliest straight plays in Broadway history up to that time.

In addition to that then-staggering sum for bringing the musical-size show to New York, the cast of 32 members and 26 different scenes depicting Auntie Mame's lavish Beekman Place apartment over a period of 18 years, resulted in an unusually high weekly operating and set-up cost for a production. During the mid-1950s, the standard top weeknight ticket price for any show was $5.75, and

$6.90 Friday and Saturday nights, so the maximum weekly box office gross at the Broadhurst could be only $42,000. After cast and stage worker salaries, investor reimbursement, theater expenses and numerous miscellaneous costs pursuant to any show, the net profit from *Auntie Mame* could only reach as much as $8,000 per week.

But, a frenzy of advance ticket sales at the box office quelled any fleeting negative notion about Mame's magnetism. The public confidently bought out every seat for every performance of this new play in Philadelphi – even before a single critic cast his coercive vote – and their confidence proved justified.

Fifteen pre-Broadway performances were scheduled for the National Theatre in Washington, D.C. with a total of 25,200 seats – but a quarter of a million playgoers demanded tickets! Jay Carmody, of the *Washington Star* commented in his review: "Humans suddenly are completely unhinged by their hunger to see a comedy as enchanting as this one starring Rosalind Russell. Ticket demand is running ten times the supply."

He concluded: "'*Auntie Mame* has everything; the absolute ideal of a stage success story: a ravishing star and a musical-sized production. It is sophisticated, sentimental, alternately riotously funny and wistful. In short, the complete comedy."

In his October 17th review, *Washington Post and Times Herald* critic Richard Coe said, "*Auntie Mame* could make us all happy by sticking around the National [Theatre] for another 83 [weeks]. Adaptors Lawrence & Lee have been wise enough to include as many of her adventurers, friends and foes as a single stage can manage. A lusty cheer to all concerned and let's see if the National can't be enlarged immediately. There's a lot of us to squeeze in before this show closes."

Exuberant public reaction and lavish critical praise, coupled with *Auntie Mame* on the *New York Times* best-seller list (77 weeks by the time of the play's opening) the stage production achieved one of the largest advance bookings for a straight play in Broadway's history.

The successful run in Washington, D.C. was capped by an invitation for Russell to dine at the White House alone with Dwight and Mamie Eisenhower on October 23. Then it was on to New York – and the ultimate test of the play's future.

*

Rosalind and company arrived in Manhattan on Saturday, October 28. Though suffering from an eye infection, Roz appeared well and happy, and was once again excited about the show.

On Sunday the cast rehearsed all day but time never allowed them a chance to do a complete run-through. Still, the cast had to face a benefit preview audience that evening.

Two previews were scheduled for New York. For the first performance, Sunday, October 29, the audience was comprised mainly of several ladies' theatre clubs. They arrived at the Broadhurst Theatre – and sat stonily throughout the show without offering nary a giggle. Performers typically loath doing theatre party performances because these houses are frequently made up of largely unenthusiastic patrons who are attending a show to mollify a spouse or support a social or charitable group.

Audiences had screamed with laughter all during the out-of-town performances. Now, in New York, they mimicked a group of manikins. Lawrence and Lee described the horrific scenario in their article, "The Remarkable Roz":

"Our preview at the Broadhurst was before a benefit audience which had not yet been told by the New York critics that it was all right to laugh. So they didn't. Timing went haywire. Moments of high comedy which had stopped the show on the road got barely a chuckle."

"You'd think we were doing a passion play during Holy

Week for all the laughs we got," muses Peggy Cass.

"Rosalind was furious," recalls Jerome Lawrence. "During intermission that night she called for the leader of one of the theatre parties that purchased tickets. 'Bring her backstage!' Russell demanded. When the woman arrived, Rosalind turned on her and screamed, 'You bitch! How dare you! How dare you just sit out there – we know this is a funny play. How dare you give us an audience that doesn't have the brains to laugh! Are you afraid your false teeth will fall out!?'" Lawrence remembers that he and the other principals all stood there mortified as the mighty star Rosalind Russell tore into the aghast – and speechless – woman.

The second preview the next night faired somewhat better, yet the tepid audience response was still far from what Russell sought. With last-minute jitters she began to question what in the hell she was doing in this show in the first place.

On October 31, 1956, rain drenched New York all day long. War broke out in Egypt, and Hungary was fighting the rampage of communism. Rosalind Russell was a nervous wreck but probably didn't even know about the world's strife – she was worrying about her own problems, specifically the New York premiere of *Auntie Mame* that night and the possibility that the show wasn't as funny as she and everyone else had anticipated.

The events of the hours before the opening night performance were a blur for everyone. The announced curtin time was 7:45 p.m. and when the house lights at the 1,155-seat Broadhurst Theatre finally dimmed, a hush fell over the starstudded audience which included Joshua Logan, Douglas Fairbanks, Mary Martin and her husband Richard Halliday, George S. Kaufman, Dorothy and Herb Fields, Doris and Jule Styne, Susan Strasberg, Ina Claire, and Annie Laurie Williams.

At curtain's rise, an austere voice off-stage read "The last Will and Testament of Edwin Dennis," the text appearing on a scrim at the proscenium: "... In the event of my demise I direct our faithful servant Norah Muldoon, to deliver Patrick to my sister and next of kin, Mame Dennis, at 3 Beekman Place, New York City ..."

The legal document was fortuitously signed on the 14th day of October 1928 and was immediately followed by a bold-faced banner of the *Chicago Tribune* dated October 15, 1928, pronouncing: "BUSINESSMAN DROPS DEAD IN THE STEAM ROOM OF THE CHICAGO ATHLETIC CLUB."

Scenes one and two of the first act introduced ten-year-old Patrick Dennis (played by Jan Handzlik), his nursemaid Norah Muldoon (Beulah Garrick) and the preliminary business of the orphaned Patrick being sent to live with his only living relative, Mame Dennis.

As scene three came up on Mame's swank Manhattan apartment – depicting a loud and garish Prohibition-era cocktail party – tremendous anticipation swelled as this sophisticated audience waited for Rosalind Russell to take the stage.

Mame Dennis (Rosalind Russell, on staircase) greets her cocktail party guests and newly arrived nephew Patrick (Jan Handzlik (center, left) and maid Nora Muldoon (Beulah Garrick, center, right), in the 1956 Broadway production of *Auntie Mame*. (Courtesy of James Monks)

At last, upstage center, atop the second floor landing of a formal staircase, her black hair bobbed short, lacquered fingernails, and a lengthy cigarette holder hanging indolently from her fiery red mouth, Rosalind Russell as Auntie Mame swept down the narrow staircase onto the stage of the Broadhurst Theatre.

The laughs throughout the evening came every ten seconds and before the safety curtain descended two and a half hours later that first night, Auntie Mame emerged to her legions of admirers as a real, live, flesh-and-blood cultural heroine, and Broadway once again belonged to Rosalind Russell.

As cast member James Monks remembered of that first night, "When the curtain finally rang down after about nine or ten curtain calls, I heard the cast applauding Rosalind Russell backstage. Practically everybody in the theatre crowded into Roz's dressing room in what looked like a *greenhouse* of flowers filling *every inch* of that room."

CHAPTER FOUR

A Star is Reborn

FOLLOWING the unforgettable opening night performance, a select cluster of VIP guests gathered at Joshua Logan's Riverside Drive apartment to salute Broadway's newest hit show and brightest star.

A *Who's Who* of Broadway notables, the invited guests paid homage to Russell, as they eagerly awaited the early reviews of the show. The atmosphere was mixed with elations and unquestionably a sense of security, for they all instinctively felt that the show was going to be a smash hit and in for a long run.

When the early editions of the New York papers arrived – literally hot-off-the-presses – the critics unanimously proclaimed the show a triumph for Russell. Her personal reviews were ecstatic and uncontested. And with the Presidential election between Dwight D. Eisenhower and Adlai E. Stevenson only days away, the *New York Times'* renowned theatre critic, Brooks Atkinson, used the ballot as an analogy for his left-handed rave review of *Auntie Mame*.

"Since neither party nominated Rosalind Russell for President, she has naturally reverted to the theatre," he wrote. "She is a special kind of comedienne, not the only one who can give a line a malicious inflection or radiate sardonicism by looking blank, but one who is also big-hearted and makes a point of getting along amiably with the human race. She is triumphantly entertaining in *Auntie Mame*."

As copies of the other papers were passed among the euphoric guests, it was evident that the hard work had paid off.

"But Darling, I'm Your Auntie Mame!" exclaims Mame Dennis (Rosalind Russell, center) as she welcomes her orphaned nephew Patrick (Jan Handzlik, right), in the 1956 Broadway production of *Auntie Mame.* Back Row: (Left to right) Polly Rowles as Vera Charles; John O'Hare as M. Lindsay Woolsey; and Grant Sullivan as Ralph Devine. (Courtesy of Jerome Lawrence).

Said John McClain of the *New York Journal-American*: "*Auntie Mame* is a towering and tremendous hit. It exceeds advance notices from the road; it is better than the book from which it was adapted. The first night audience at the Broadhurst, where it opened last night and figures to remain indefinitely, spent a rigorous evening rocking with laughter and occasionally dabbing at their eyes. The Jerome Lawrence-Robert E. Lee version of Patrick Dennis's best-selling novel has added a strong element of 'heart' to the original story. It took quite some time to bring us a bright new success, but it is worth waiting for."

The *Daily Mirror*'s Robert Coleman raved, "With Rosalind Russell up, *Auntie Mame* breezed home a winner at the Broadhurst Wednesday evening. What a grand and glorious ride she gave the Jerome Lawrence-Robert E. Lee comedy champ. Using a laugh here and a heart-throb there, she turned in one of the most terrific performances glimpsed on the Main Stem track in many a season. Lawrence and Lee have fashioned a thunderbolt of fun from the Patrick Dennis best-seller."

Roz, however, was not as delighted with her performance as the critics and audiences. "I'd scarcely bothered about my own part," she recalled in her autobiography. "All the time I'd worked with Tec [DaCosta], my concentration had been on other things, because if everybody isn't good, if somebody's dragging the play down every other line, if the material isn't there, you're in trouble. Then, with the audience already out there waiting, I thought, I don't know what I'm doing. I knew where I was going, yes, but I really was not as good in *Auntie Mame* on opening night as I had been in *Wonderful Town*. Still, what the audience didn't know didn't hurt them."

*

"I really did not know if *Auntie Mame* would be a hit,"

recalled Morton DaCosta. "It's almost like a musical. In fact, a lot of people remember it as a musical because it is episodic. I had a lot of questions. I knew it would amuse an audience, but I didn't know how it would fare critically."

For his part, author Patrick Dennis praised the playwrights when the printed version of the play was published by Vanguard Press. In a touching introduction, the author stated: "Having had nothing to do with writing the play *Auntie Mame* it is easy for me to be quite detached and objective about it. All I can say, right along with the critics and the thousands of people who have seen it, is that it makes a wonderfully entertaining evening in the theatre. Lawrence and Lee have caught – far better than I – the moments of heartbreak that are also in *Auntie Mame* and placed them on stage so deftly that, between the guffaws and sniffles, snickers and snorts, there are audible sobs and visible tears at each and every performance."

This was an unusual acknowledgment by an author. Generally it seems novelists feel that their work has been diminished, defiled and mutilated by the unfeeling souls who transfer their work to the stage or screen.

In the light of day following the opening, Rosalind was, not surprisingly, utterly exhausted. She was elated about her personal reviews but had expected better critical notices for the supporting cast. However, the advance sale of tickets had topped the $1 million mark and she was ecstatic and pleased.

Financial backers were calling the show *My Fair Mame*, an amusing twist on another hit, *My Fair Lady*. Gossip columnist Sheilah Graham reported that the *Auntie Mame* production required 15 people to handle the deluge of mail-order ticket requests; newspaper ads advised that when writing in for tickets that five alternate dates to see the show should be included.

Producer Robert Fryer remembers that the demand for seats was so enormous that the company's general manager, Benjamin

Franklin Stein, did some rather creative seating arrangements in the balcony. "At the Broadhurst Theatre there is no second balcony, just little coves. In order to get more people into the theatre, Ben called this area 'The Queens Box.' He put chairs up there and charged *more* money for tickets to those spaces," the producer smiles.

With unanimous rave reviews for *Auntie Mame* and a million-dollar advance at the box office, it was time to settle down for a long run of the show.

Playwright Sumner Locke Elliott – who had been treated so poorly during the early phases of the production, finally saw the production and sent a note to Russell, praising the play and her performance. "Lawrence and Lee did an excellent job," he wrote. "It was exactly as it should have been."

Russell replied to Elliott's gracious note and acknowledged that it was entirely her fault that he had been led up the garden path the year before. "That was very satisfactory to me," Elliott says.

※

Hit plays are not all smooth sailing however, and *Auntie Mame* was no exception. Shortly after the play opened, an all-girl college in Virginia wrote a letter to the producers requesting a change in the script.

"It is our understanding that one of the characters, Gloria Upson, is a student or former student, at Sweet Briar, and that her remarks reflect unfavorably upon Sweet Briar," one faculty member wrote. "We understand that the impression created on many members of the play's large audiences is unjustly harmful because of the strong prejudices expressed by the young woman who is purported to be a Sweet Briar student."

To avoid any further conflict with the school or undue negative publicity, the writers agreed to replace the name "Sweet

Briar" with the name of a fictional institution.

Perhaps the most bizarre legal matter facing *Auntie Mame* involved a law suit filed by Raymond Duncan, brother of then deceased internationally acclaimed dancer Isadora Duncan, against Jerome Lawrence, Robert E. Lee, Robert Fryer, Lawrence Carr, actor Cris Alexander and Vanguard Press.

Raymond Duncan was often a figure of public satire, and this time he brought suit in the Supreme Court of the State of New York alleging that he suffered damages from the use of a character in the play named Raymond. His complaint was that the character was attired in a manner worn by him and the reference in the dialogue to Isadora Duncan was damaging to him.

Cris Alexander, who played the part of Raymond in the play remembers, "I used to see him [Duncan] boarding the 57th Street bus with his toga and thongs. I think he wanted the publicity and would like to have had some money because he was always struggling [to make ends meet]."

In response to the plaintiff's charge of defamation, Jerry Lawrence countered the ludicrous allegations stating that, "Duncan is not shown as drinking in the play, he is not shown as doing anything which the real Mr. Duncan doesn't do."

When consulted on the matter Edward Tanner expressed his thoughts that it would be a big mistake to settle the case without a fight. But the defendants decided they would rather settle the matter without litigation. Feeling that the expense of winning a lawsuit would probably be more costly than settling, they also wanted to avoid taking the time which could be devoted to more creative matters.

In an out-of-court settlement, the producers paid $3,500 to Raymond Duncan. In addition, Vanguard Press agreed that in connection with any future printing of the book or play *Auntie Mame*, there would be a deletion of the names Raymond

Duncan, Isadora and Isadora Duncan. It was also agreed that the name Raymond would be changed to Oswald and that the name Isadora would be changed to Daphne. Also the costume worn by the character formerly known as Raymond would be something other than the white linen toga worn by Duncan.

*

It was said that in the play *Auntie Mame* the laughs come every ten seconds. Indeed, Peggy Cass remembers on three separate occasions pregnant women had to be rushed to the hospital because their laughing brought on labor. And stalwart Rosalind Russell never missed a single performance, which must have been a source of consternation for her standby, Haila Stoddard, who would eventually get her chance – but not while Rosalind Russell was in the show.

Each night following her thunderous ovations and curtain calls, Russell tucked up the filmy sari which she wore in her final scene and made a beeline for her dressing room just past the stage door at the Broadhurst Theatre. On days with matinee performances she was on stage for five hours and six minutes, and battled her way through 28 complete costume and hairdo changes. By midnight the star was back in her suite at the Hotel Pierre, in her bathrobe.

Every Friday night while Russell was starring as Auntie Mame, her son Lance would come to the theatre. "I was in school at the time and I remember she would have me go out and count the standees," he recalls. "I'm not really sure why she did that, she may have been double-checking to make sure the grosses were being added correctly – but we had a code language – she would ask me to go out and count the 'candies.'"

A hit play produces a grueling schedule for its cast members and *Auntie Mame* was no exception. With only a week off in April, Russell found the eight shows per week a difficult grind. However,

87

it must have been equally trying for young Jan Handzlik, who had to balance his stage career with compulsory academic studies.

"I went to a school that was designed for children in the theatre," Handzlik recalls. "We lived in Waukegan, New Jersey on the bluffs overlooking the Hudson and Manhattan. Each morning I took the bus to the Port Authority terminal and then took the subway to school. After class I would return home and then come back to Manhattan for the evening performance."

And when the curtain came down late each night after the performance, Master Handzlik took the train home alone.

"I was really well taken care of," the young actor-turned-lawyer recalls. "My mother had arranged for a Port Authority policeman to meet me at the steps of the subway station on 44th

Joyce Lear (right) as simpleminded society girl Gloria Upson, whose impending nuptials to Patrick Dennis (Robert Higgins, center) has Auntie Mame (Rosalind Russell, left) scheming to alter their plans, in the original 1956 Broadway production of *Auntie Mame*. (Courtesy of Jerome Lawrence)

Street after each performance. At 44th and 8th there are steps that lead down to a long underground passage and goes all the way to the Port Authority bus terminal. The policeman would meet me there after the play and we'd walk to the bus station together," he says reassuringly.

*

The show was a smash hit, seats were sold-out months in advance, and Russell, as a result, had the two producers wrapped around her long, slender fingers. When it came time for the producers to coax her into extending her contract, she used her clout.

On February 6, 1957, *Daily Variety* reported that Russell was making huge demands as a concession to her remaining in the show. As the star attraction, she knew she had enormous leverage and she insisted that the production close during the hot summer months of July and August. She also insisted that the producers pay her vacation transportation expenses to and from the West Coast, that they pay the rent on her New York hotel suite during her absence and increase the promotion and billboard budgets by $1,000 per week.

The major point for negotiation, however, was that Russell insisted that the producers pay her a $25,000 signing bonus for continuing in the show. She was adamant, however, that the money not come from the production itself (she was an investor with a 13.43% share) but from Fryer and Carr's own pockets, to be deposited in escrow for five years, in order to avoid significant taxation.

"She took the gold out of our teeth in order to get her to continue in that show," Fryer reportedly remarked several years later.

The terms were seemingly met, but, after a fifteen-month run, the producers announced the star would be leaving the cast as of January 18, 1958. She would then go to Hollywood for the motion picture adaptation of the play.

There had been much speculation about the show continuing without Rosalind Russell in the title role. Because of all the *Auntie Mame* publicity centered around her, it was feared that it would be impossible to replace her. It was suggested to Fryer and Carr that not only would they be unable to find a replacement, but that they would never find anyone to take the show on the road. "At least I doubt if you will get a name actress who would be able to fit the role properly," one theater insider advised. "My prediction is that when Miss Russell leaves the show the play will close and that there will never be a road show of this play at all!"

After the stock market crash, Mame Dennis (Rosalind Russell) is swept away by rich and handsome Beauregard Jackson Picket Burnside (Robert Smith), in the 1956 Broadway production of *Auntie Mame*. (Courtesy of James Monks)

That insider could have been Rosalind Russell herself. As Jerome Lawrence remembers, Russell was very proprietary about Auntie Mame and didn't think anyone else should do the role on Broadway and that the show should thus close upon her departure. "We told her how wrong she was, and that if for no other reason than the fact that she was an investor in the show, it should continue to run," recalls Lawrence. "She got quite angry and said, 'I'm an investor in my part too!'"

The hostile debate about closing the Broadway production of Auntie Mame turned out to be one of the reasons why Lawrence and Lee were not offered the plum assignment of adapting their own stage play into a screenplay for the motion picture version of the show. "It was partly because Roz was furious with us for letting anyone else play the part," says Lawrence.

"After the play was a huge hit and she was ready to do the film, she went to Fryer and Carr and said, 'Well, naturally you're going to close the play,' Lawrence continues. "They actually might have considered it, but Morton DaCosta, Bob [Lee] and I went to them and said, 'Don't you dare close this! This is a gold mine and there are a lot of other women who could play it!' They said they felt kind of obligated to Roz because she made it such a hit.

"'She didn't make it a hit!,' we retorted. 'She helped make it a hit because she was sensational in it. But a lot of other women would be equally sensational!'

"So, we personally flew to Santa Fe, New Mexico, and talked to Greer Garson about doing the play," Lawrence says. "We had seen her do a comedy bit on *The Steve Allen Show*. That was the clincher.

"Roz was absolutely furious and wouldn't talk to us for a year," Lawrence says.

Dorothy Blackburn recalls that after *Auntie Mame* opened and became a smash hit, she cornered Robert Fryer after a performance one night and said, "I suppose you'll be sending out another company soon."

"Oh, we couldn't do that," Fryer responded. "We have the only person who can play Auntie Mame right here on Broadway – Rosalind Russell."

Blackburn remembers that about a month later, three young men: Charles Bowden, Richard Barr and H. Ridgely Bullock Jr., made arrangements to form a road company of *Auntie Mame*.

"Everybody said, 'Oh, those poor young men! No one else can play the character,'" Blackburn remembers. "It was Constance Bennett who was selected to do that part for the first road company and we all watched for the opening in Cleveland. Much to everybody's surprise, the reviews were absolute raves! Then, one after another, other companies opened. Every one was a complete success with equally rave reviews!"

After losing her fortune in the stock market crash of 1929, Mame (Rosalind Russell) takes a series of menial jobs, including switchboard operator, in the original 1956 Broadway production of *Auntie Mame*. (Courtesy of Jerome Lawrence).

Prior to Miss Bennett opening in Boston, one of the stops on her tour, playwrights Lawrence and Lee were informed by letter that the chaste city officials of Bean Town would not allow the actress to utter the words God, Lord or Jesus Christ. Charles Bowden, one of the producers of the road company wrote, "On opening night we will not cut any of the sons-of-bitches, but do feel – since we are always forewarned before opening in Boston – that we must make substitutions for the other areas."

*

On the night of Russell's final performance in *Auntie Mame*, she sent a telegram to the entire cast as a good luck cheer for the upcoming first performance without her: "I READ WEBSTER ALL NIGHT, AND A LITTLE PROUST TOO, FOR WAYS OF EXPRESSING HOW MUCH I LOVE YOU AND TO FIND SOME NEW WORDS TO TELL YOU HOW GRATEFUL I AM FOR YOUR FABULOUS GIFT TO THIS LONESOME OLD HAM. I LIFT MY GLASS AND TOAST THAT I'VE WORKED WITH THE BEST. GOOD LUCK TONIGHT AND KNOW THAT MY HEART IS RIGHT THERE... A WEE BIT OF LIGHT AT THE TOP OF THE STAIRS."

Russell's closing night in *Auntie Mame* was even more exciting and heartfelt than her opening. For the occasion, as the curtain rang down on her farewell performance, the entire company remained on stage while Roz acknowledged her ovation from the jam-packed Broadhurst. In a beautiful curtain speech, free of maudlin sentiment, but emotionally sincere, she expressed her deep gratitude to everyone who helped contribute to the success of the production. Then, she made a touching acknowledgment of her lovely successor, Greer Garson.

Backstage, the cast presented Russell with a magnificent crystal and sterling silver ice bucket. Producers Fryer and Carr gifted her with an engraved sterling silver cigarette box from Cartier; and Lawrence & Lee gave her a large Mark Cross scrapbook with "Auntie Mame" emblazoned in gold.

Roz changed clothes and joined her *Auntie Mame* family at The Coat of Arms, a bistro owned by cast member Bob Smith who played Beauregard.

That night Robert Fryer toasted: "In the old days they used to refer to Bernhardt as "The divine Sarah." Today we refer to "The divine Rosalind."

"In terms of her professional life, I think *Auntie Mame* had to be among the most satisfying experiences for my mother," notes Lance Brisson. "People have always asked me, was your mother like Auntie Mame. The truthful answer, in my view, is that she had some characteristics of Mame but there were many that she didn't have. My mother was not an eccentric person, she was a very practical, New England, down-to-earth person. They shared such traits as a sense of independence and unwillingness to be pigeon holed or restricted by life. A joy of living that Auntie Mame exemplified."

*

Greer Garson, the cinematic epitome of dignity, nobility and beauty of mature womanhood, and star of such classic films as *Random Harvest, Goodbye, Mr. Chips, Madame Curie, Blossoms in the Dust* and *Mrs. Miniver,* began rehearsals for *Auntie Mame* on December 23, 1957, and made her Broadway debut on January 20, 1958. To some, Garson's beauty was so luminous that it was easier to believe that the character Beauregard would fall instantly in love with her. Where Roz was a handsome woman, Garson had some added magic that made her more believable in the touching, quieter moments of the play.

On January 20, 1958, Academy Award-winner Greer Garson (second from right) replaced Rosalind Russell as the star of Broadway's hit comedy, *Auntie Mame*. Also starring with her are (left to right) Grant Sullivan, Polly Rowles, John O'Hare and Jan Handzlik. (Courtesy of Jerome Lawrence)

Polly Rowles (left) as sodden actress Vera Charles, with Academy Award-winner Greer Garson (right) as Auntie Mame. (Courtesy of Jerome Lawrence)

"I thought Rosalind Russell was a brilliant comedienne and played all the comedy magnificently," recalls James Monks who portrayed Brian O'Bannion. "But frankly, I also thought that Miss Garson added another dimension of warmth in the Christmas Depression scene,"

Shortly after Rosalind left the show, Peggy Cass, Yuki Shimoda and Jan Handzlik followed suit and went to California to appear in the motion picture *Auntie Mame.*

"So many of us were left back," recalls Monks. "It was a real double-cross because we were told by Tec DaCosta that he would send for us once he got things going on the Coast. He knew damn well he wasn't going to send for us because it was in Miss Garson's contract that she could have some key people from the original company. I think we made her feel more comfortable."

Indeed, Garson had signed to do the role of Mame Dennis with the proviso that Robert Smith and others *not* be released to do the movie. Smith recalls, "I had heard that I was the only one they were considering for the movie version, so I just sat and waited thinking I could sneak out for a couple of weeks and do my part as Beauregard. It would have been a big leg up in my career. Then I found out that Greer would not have me released. This didn't enchant me, but I loved Greer and we were good friends, so I didn't let it bother me too much."

It was said that the winter of 1958 was the coldest and most grim in New York since 1919. The freezing "Montreal Express" whipping down from Canada, and the warm radiators giving off essential heat in the dressing rooms, provided a fertile atmosphere for illness at the Broadhurst Theatre.

"I was neatly sabotaged by the Shubert painters who used old-fashioned oil paint on my actual opening day to repaint the entire dressing room," grieved Garson in a letter to Robert E. Lee. "When I came in there were two stoves and a radiator blasting away – so it was really like a torture chamber. I don't know how I got on that Monday as I was so nauseated and choked up, and the next day I had a raging sore throat and the voice began to give at the edges."

That Wednesday morning, Garson awoke to find she had no voice at all. She spent the day with an ear-nose-throat specialist and voice therapist. This was the only time that Auntie Mame standby Haila Stoddard had a chance to go on stage in the title role. And it was the only time in Garson's career that she had missed performances (a total of 8), but it was unavoidable. "I battled a virus and often played with a high temperature," she said.

But there were many fond memories for Garson to take away from her involvement in *Auntie Mame*. Perhaps the most rewarding was the kinship she developed with an unlikely group of admirers – the *New York Times* printers. The stage door of the Broadhurst Theatre is just across the street from the loading docks of the *Times*, and every evening Greer Garson would come through the stage door a few minutes after the printers had come up from the pressroom caverns for their nightly coffee break.

As one *New York Times* report noted: "Greer Garson would come through the stage door, the pressmen would wave and she would wave back as she stepped into her waiting limousine. This became a ritual and each night as the limo pulled away she would throw kisses. The chauffeur added a touch of his own. Pulling away from the curb he would blink his headlights as the car rolled slowly past the *Times'* loading platforms in the eastbound street.

"All through February, March, April and the first two weeks in May, the kisses and blinking lights and rather shy salute from the inky 13 kept up. Not a word was exchanged between Greer Garson and her besumdged worshipers. But on a Monday night, May 12, the chauffeur came across the street with a Broadhurst Theatre envelope. In it was a note from Miss Garson's hand addressed: 'To my boys at the *New York Times* Building on West 44th Street.'

"The note read, 'My Dear Boys: I'll be leaving West 44th Street soon but I'll have so many happy memories – and I'll never forget your friendly 'goodnight salutes.' I look forward to that every evening. Have a drink with Auntie Mame. With love and best wishes to each and every one of you, Greer Garson.'

"With the note came a bottle of Bourbon and a bottle of Scotch. The night after the note and whiskey came, the 13 pressmen chipped in for three and a half dozen pink roses. Each pressman put his inky signature to the card that went with the bouquet. On May 14, the actress sent an answer to the gift – 13 autographed photos. They had proof of their romance, to bring home to doubting wives and sweethearts."

At the conclusion of Greer Garson's Broadway run in *Auntie Mame*, another major star essayed the role of Mame Dennis at the Broadhurst Theatre. Beatrice Lillie opened on June 2, for four weeks, in preparation for her opening in the London company produced by David Pelham.

Other international stars such as Margaret Leighton, Gloria Swanson, Mary Martin, Claudette Colbert and June Havoc had been pursued for the London edition of the show, but each had reasons to ultimately decline. In Miss Havoc's case, there was a British ruling about pets having to be quarantined for six months prior to being allowed entry into the country. "Some things mean more to me than applause," she said, "namely my fur people," which was how she referred to her pets.

British talent agent Lillie Messenger had also called Lawrence & Lee about her client Sarah Churchill (daughter of the Prime Minister) being available and eager to do the London production. In a written response to their publisher, the two playwrights facetiously replied, "We are lukewarm about this, that is unless Sir Winston plays Ito."

Long acknowledged as one of the most brilliant comic geniuses of the 20th century, Beatrice Lillie began her legendary career in the 1920s, in *Charlot's Revue*, a London success that subsequently established her as a star on Broadway. By the time she became Auntie Mame in 1958, her outrageous bent for lunacy had been showcased in such musical comedies as *She's My Baby, This Year of Grace, The Third Little Show* (in which she introduced "Mad Dogs and Englishmen"), *At Home Abroad, The Show Is On, Inside U.S.A.* and Shaw's *Too True to be Good*, among other top musicals. And when Beatrice Lillie took over as the mad woman of Beekman Place, she dazzled audiences and critics alike, scoring another personal and professional triumph.

James Monks remembers the enormous excitement he experienced working with the world's most celebrated clown, and describes his first encounter thus: "When she came in for our first rehearsal, I made my entrance to nephew Patrick's dialogue line, 'There's a Mr. O'Bannion to see you.' Auntie Mame turns around, takes one look at this hunk – I'm speaking objectively – and says, 'Do come in Mr. O'Bannion.'

"Of course I adored Lillie, and loved everything she had ever done – and I just fell apart laughing when she spoke that line. I couldn't control myself. [Stage manager] Bob Linden was in a rage. I went back to make my entrance again…and broke up a second time.

"I apologized to Bob and the company and said, 'I'm sorry, but I have worshipped this woman and her readings for so long, and to find myself on the same stage with her is just too much.' They gave me a third chance and I finally played it well."

Monks wasn't alone in his adoration of Beatrice Lillie. Even those who weren't worshipers conceded and applauded her brilliance. In his review of Lillie's first performance as Auntie Mame, critic Brooks Atkinson noted that "She began so diffidently that customers who had just left $6.90 in the box office took the liberty of screaming 'louder.' It was her first performance before an audience, and not a fair sample of what she can do when she is under full sail with the wind in the right quarter."

But, Atkinson was quick to advise, "Even a ragged performance by Miss Lillie is entertaining, her mind works so fast and makes such quick thought transference to the audience that an occasional fluff became funny and an accident with a wig looked like a fresh antic that the director had not thought of. When the final curtain came down the audience was shouting 'brava' as though Duse had just upstaged Bernhardt.'"

The "wig incident," as the situation was referred to, became a funny gag that helped make *Auntie Mame* "Auntie Bea's" own. Jerome Lawrence remembers, "At one performance her wig fell off and she got such a laugh that she let it fall during other performances. She did another piece of business where she drops the terrible *hors d'oeuvre* that Mrs. Upson serves. Instead of tossing it over her shoulder as originally directed, she stepped on it and did a little pirouette when her hostess wasn't looking, crushing it into crumbs."

Other punctuations to the role, as only Beatrice Lillie could conceive, were equally legendary. For instance, at the end of the first act, when she catches the "fox" after the debilitating side saddle horseback ride in the hunt, Bea deftly made the tuckered little creature into a fur seat and lowered her sore bottom on to it.

"She got the biggest scream I have ever heard in the theatre," Lawrence recalls of that incident. "This was all her doing. She never changed a line of dialogue, but she did create some almost Chaplinesque type business."

"She was my idol," says Polly Rowles. "She was the funniest woman who ever lived – and one of the most original. But she had never memorized anything like this before and we never knew what would happen when she was on stage. But the audience was never aware of anything going wrong. She kept the cast on their toes when she was on stage."

However, some of the cast found Beatrice Lillie (née Lady Peel, widow of Sir Robert Peel who died in 1934) rather distant: "She wasn't friendly," recalls Robert Smith. "In the Peckerwood Plantation scene at the end of the fox hunt, she comes on stage, I propose to her and we are to have a big embrace. When I would go to embrace her she would put both hands up and hold me off. I was furious! It made me look like a jerk. I went to the producers and told them I wanted to rehearse that scene until she could do it properly. So they called a special rehearsal. Very seldom can you do that with a star, but they called it anyway."

Lillie's excuse for her behavior, according to Smith, was that she suffered a great deal of physical pain. "I have bursitis so bad I can't raise my arms," he recalls her saying.

"So we had to restage the scene so that I had my back to the audience and they couldn't see that she was holding me off with her hands. She wasn't fun for me to work with," Smith concludes.

By the time Lillie crossed the Atlantic and ensconced herself at the Adelphi Theatre in London's West End, she had the character down pat. Despite her critical triumph in New York however, the most influential paper in the U.K., The *London Times*, failed to see what all the fuss in the States was about. The theatre critic whose byline was Hobson, completely dismissed the star and the production.

Producer David Pelham was an inspired man of the theatre. In a brilliant take on the situation, he created an advertising sandwich board and placed it outside the theatre. It announced:

"TOTAL DISASTER" — Hobson, *Times*. THIS PERFORMANCE TOTALLY SOLD-OUT!

For once, the public paid little attention to what the nay-saying arbiter of entertainment suggested was unworthy of their support, and the production became a long-running hit in the same league as *My Fair Lady*.

For every actress who portrayed Auntie Mame, a different and equally strong quality of character emerged. Rosalind Russell was the quintessence of professionalism. Greer Garson brought her enormous British charm, Sylvia Sidney was the most tearful and Beatrice Lillie was a brilliant inventive clown.

In addition to the Broadway ladies in the role of Mame, Constance Bennett was touring in one road company and Eve Arden was being courted to open in the West Coast edition of the play.

In California, *Auntie Mame* starring Eve Arden and featuring Benay Venuta as Vera Charles, went into rehearsal at the Musicians Hall on Vine Street in Los Angeles, Monday, July 21, 1958, in preparation for its premiere at Russ Auditorium in San Diego on August 4.

After a critically acclaimed week in San Diego, the aggregation, which featured several members of the Broadway company including Dorothy Blackburn and Florence MacMichael (who had replaced Polly Rowles), headed to the Biltmore Theatre in Los Angeles for what would become, at that time, the highest-grossing play in the city's history, before going on to even greater success at the Geary Theatre in San Francisco.

The reviews in Los Angeles were so ecstatic for the play and the star, that Eve Arden printed facsimile copies of every one of them as the centerfold of her autobiography *The Three Phases of Eve*. Who could blame the beloved star this modest bit of self-aggrandizement; they were the kinds of reviews every actor would love to receive.

As the *Hollywood Reporter* declared, "Even Arden again demonstrates that in the fine art of the double-take long sidelong glance, she has few peers. Additionally, she brings to the part the important element of warmth, without which Auntie Mame becomes a freak."

Daily Variety touted, "...this is a triumphant return to the stage for Miss Arden, confined in recent years almost exclusively to the limiting dimensions of the 21-inch screen, and it appears likely that she'll set new box office records at the Biltmore in her eight-week run.

"As for Miss Arden's dynamic contribution, on physical demands alone it's enormous. She changes moods as swiftly and blithely as she does costumes and wigs (seven of the latter). She is bawdy, tender, brazen and romantic, and in all she is bewitching, funny and believable."

Patterson Greene summed it up best in his review for the *Los Angeles Examiner*. "Many of Miss Arden's lines are like tinseled hand grenades, and she tosses them with split-second timing and unerring aim. Best of all, she never departs into caricature. Her Auntie Mame is warm, winning and true, and her swift excursions in and out of pathos and sentimentality are as delectable as her wit and ribaldry."

CHAPTER FIVE

Auntie Mame in Hollywood

THE TELEGRAM to young Jan Handzlik simply read: DEAR LITTLE PATRICK: NOW WASH YOUR HANDS AND COMB YOUR HAIR AND BE MY OWN DARLING NEPHEW ALL OVER AGAIN. GOOD LUCK. AUNTIE MAME.

Much to the resentment of other cast members, only Handzlik, Peggy Cass and Yuki Shimoda were invited from the Broadway success to join director Morton DaCosta and Rosalind Russell for the Warner Bros. film adaptation of "Auntie Mame." The others were to remain in New York and continue to perform with Greer Garson.

On the night of January 24, 1958, Rosalind Russell and her maid, Blanche Williams, left New York by rail aboard the Super Chief, and arrived in Los Angeles the morning of January 27, to report to the Warner Bros. studio in Burbank.

Pre-production on the motion picture *Auntie Mame* began in early January, even before Russell left her duties with the Broadway play. For a straight salary of $150,000, Warner Bros. was getting the toast of Broadway to star in one of the strongest pre-sold properties to come to the screen in years.

While that salary is a pittance by today's vastly inflated standards, in 1958 it was enormous compensation. Based on the success of *Auntie Mame* in New York and the high expectations for the film, the studio counted on this hot property to show a profit and salvage the studio which in recent years had fallen on hard times.

Warner Bros. was a stalwart of the motion picture business. However, in the mid-1950s, Hollywood was in financial straits. The studio that introduced talking pictures was falling on hard times. According to *The Warner Bros. Story*, Clive Hirschhorn's definitive history of the studio, the studio showed a net loss of $1,023,000 in 1957, the year before *Auntie Mame* came to the screen.

The plight of Warner Bros.' dire financial condition was implied in a memo to studio executive Steve Trilling on January 29, 1958. A seemingly simple request from Russell to hire her favorite make-up artist, Gene Hibbs, at his regular salary of $450 per week created a stir. The studio refused to pay what seemed to them a large chunk of money for his services, and as a result Russell had to cough up the balance between what the studio would cover ($350 per week) and what she felt Hibbs was entitled to receive.

"This is, of course, an outrageous salary for painting one gal's puss," the memo's author whined. "Sooner or later these hold-up birds [Russell] will find that they are killing the goose that lays the golden egg!" the writer said. "Damned if that isn't the truth when we are all striving to cut costs," he concluded.

When Robert Fryer and Jimmy Carr first purchased the rights to the Patrick Dennis novel three years earlier, they solicited the financial backing of Warner Bros. with the pledge that Warners would be the studio to make the motion picture version of the play. With the release of such Warner Bros. bombs as *X The Unknown* with Dean Jagger, and *The Story of Mankind* starring Ronald Coleman and supported by Vincent Price, Hedy Lamarr, Groucho Marx, Peter Lorre and Virgina Mayo, the studio was desperate for a hit. *Auntie Mame* was certainly not a "sure thing" when they agreed to become investors in the Broadway play, but their investment proved more than sound.

Though the deal initially did not include the specific services

Rosalind Russell as Auntie Mame, the greatest triumph of her auspicious career.

of Rosalind Russell (Eve Arden was suggested as the ideal Auntie Mame for the screen), after the play became a smash hit, it was easy enough for Fryer and Carr to convince the studio to rustle up Russell.

Interestingly, Rosalind Russell re-creating her stage role on film remains one of the very few times that the star of a Broadway show was offered the chance to reprise her triumph in the Hollywood film adaptation. Ethel Merman was never given the opportunity to do the movie based on her hits *Annie Get Your Gun, DuBarry Was a Lady, Panama Hattie, Something For the Boys* or *Gypsy* (Frederick Brisson bought the motion picture rights to the latter for his wife), Julie Andrews wasn't offered *My Fair Lady,* and Mary Martin didn't do *The Sound of Music* or *South Pacific.*

At the penultimate phase of Rosalind Russell's Broadway run in *Auntie Mame,* it was announced that the noted writing team of Betty Comden and Adolph Green had been hired by Warner Bros. to write the script.

As the motion picture freely lifts dialogue and situations and is nearly identical in structure to the play. One wonders why Jerome Lawrence and Robert E. Lee were not at least partly credited with the screenplay.

Several stories proliferate the answer to this question, not the least of which is the notion that the two authors of the play and star Rosalind Russell had a rift when the writers insisted that the play remain open on Broadway upon Russell's departure for Hollywood.

"She (Rosalind Russell) was so anxious for us to do it," recalls the celebrated Betty Comden of being assigned to write the screenplay. "We didn't know why she wanted us. We had done *Wonderful Town* with her, and we were crazy about Roz, and she liked us. She actually said she wanted us to change it a lot.

Naturally, she wanted the things left in that had been sure-fire. So we had to keep all that. We made some changes and just hoped it would flow like a movie."

The screenplay adaptation also tried to tuck in several new scenes. "We had her going other places to look for work," writer Adolph Green remembers of Mame's Depression-era endeavors.

"Yes," Comden chimes in, "she tried to run the house, tried to get a job as a cook somewhere. There were several job hunting expeditions which all ended up horribly for her."

Adolph Green remembers one of their most creative contributions being the hydraulically operated furniture in Mame's Beekman Place apartment during the last party. "We invented the rising and falling chairs for the last sequence," he says.

"There were the chairs going up and down, and other things to discomfort these prejudiced horrible people [the Upsons] and show Patrick the right road," Comden adds, speaking about Mame's determination to open her nephew's eyes to the sort of family he was marrying into.

In reviewing the final Comden & Green screenplay, the Warner Bros. censors were uneasy about several portions of the dialogue. All were lines from the play or book. "In light of the litigation we have already had with one of the Marx Brothers, perhaps we will want to eliminate this reference to them," one censor said regarding the dialogue of little Patrick's question about Karl Marx: "Is he one of the Marx Brothers?" They were also uneasy about the maid Norah Muldoon's dialogue where she announces: "The first lady of the American Theatre is out cold in the guest room," referring to sodden stage star Vera Charles. They were afraid this might be damaging to Helen Hayes who in real-life was regarded as "The First Lady of the American Theatre."

Towards the close of March, 1958, with the start of principal photography to begin in just a few days, director Morton

DaCosta had yet to cast Auntie Mame's best friend Vera Charles. Many actresses had been screen-tested for the part, including Vivian Vance – from *I Love Lucy* television fame.

"Olives take up too much room in such a little glass!" admonishes Auntie Mame (Rosalind Russell) as she teaches her adopted nephew Patrick (Jan Handzlik) to mix the perfect martini.

But DaCosta had someone very special in mind. He recalled a memorable production of *Macbeth* produced by the Old Vic Company at the Winter Garden Theatre in New York, and specifically he remembered a brilliant British actress in the play: Coral Browne.

Browne was living in London, and a copy of the script was sent to her. She liked what she read and, as she was eager to work in Hollywood, Browne accepted the assignment to portray Vera. A travel visa was issued to her on March 28th, and arrangements for her to fly to the States were made. Taking the polar route aboard Pan American flight #123, Browne left England March 30, and arrived in New York on the 31st. Her flight to Los Angeles would take yet another day, and an exhausted Browne appeared on the "Auntie Mame" set April 2 – two days into shooting.

Browne remembers, "For me, the atmosphere became chaotic because the day before I was due on the set the hairdresser dyed my hair from dark brown to platinum blonde and it all fell out overnight on the pillow! I arrived on the set bald!"

Coincidentally, the script dialogue reverberated that calamity. When Mame is preparing to meet Mr. Babcock, the stuffed-shirt banker and Trustee of Patrick's estate, she is frantically searching through dozens of wigs for an appropriate color. Vera asks, "Don't you ever throw anything away?" To which Mame responds, "Who knows when I might go back to one of these colors." Vera sarcastically fires back, "If you kept your hair natural the way I do, you wouldn't need…"

"If I kept my hair natural the way you do, I'd be bald!" Mame retorts.

The damage to Browne's hair was evaluated by a doctor and her head was treated and bound. "Costume designer Orry Kelly had to quickly improvise a turban, and I played my first scene in this way," Browne remembers.

Academy Award-winning art director Malcome Bert was hired to create the eye-catching sets. Stage #18 on the Warner Bros. lot in Burbank was dressed and decorated six different times by the studio craftsmen, with startling variations on Auntie Mame's fabulous Beekman Place apartment which seemed to change as frequently as she altered her hairstyles.

One of the most fantastic and expensive living room sets designed for the picture was Auntie Mame's Danish Modern decor for the final party sequence. The startling effect of the furnishings commenced with the view of a formidable light fixture suspended from the ceiling in the hall outside Mame's apartment. Swimming in the lamp were gold fish.

The living room itself featured "elevator furniture," hydraulically operated benches, which could be raised and lowered from a master switch at Mame's disposal. Just as the snobby Upsons are recovering from the first impact of the startling decor, they try to relax on the sofa only to be zoomed ceilingward on the hydraulically-controlled furniture.

Joanna Barnes, who was cast as Gloria Upson recalls, "We shot the scene in Mame's literary salon set on a Friday, and the minute we wrapped and closed the doors that night the crews tunneled under the stage and installed the pneumatic equipment for the modern furniture. Monday morning everything was in. The furniture went up and down. It was just amazing that they were able to do that."

Recalling how she came to be cast in what became one of the most hilarious and memorable lampoons of an empty-headed society debutante, Barnes says, "I got into *Auntie Mame* in a wonderful way. I was under contract to Warners and I was doing a film with Jean Simmons for [director] Mervyn Leroy, called 'Home Before Dark.' Mervyn came to me and said, 'You have a day off coming up and they want you to test for this part of Gloria.'

"I was a Boston debutante and did all that social register stuff. We – my family – had always sent up the ditzy version of these people. When I had gone away to school, my mother, in Boston, said to me, 'Just don't come back with a hot potato in your mouth.' So of course I used to call her and tease her with (an affectionate)'Hello Mums.'

"So I went to meet Morton DaCosta and used that voice. He liked it and had me screen-tested. I knew people like Gloria. So to play one was just perfect heaven, and so many times since, I have heard take-offs on Gloria, done in clubs."

Barnes kidded herself by playing another variation on Gloria Upson (voice and all) in Walt Disney Pictures' 1961 live-action comedy, *The Parent Trap.*

*

Regaining terra firma, the Upsons' ruffled feelings are supposed to be soothed by Flaming Mame cocktails. They make abortive attempts to bring the cups close to their faces, but the fire in each glass is too much of a hazard. The studio special effects department was called in to concoct a fluid that would burn with a red flame. The transparent blue flame from pure alcohol could scarcely be picked up by the motion picture camera. The effect was accomplished by mixing synthetic alcohol and sterno.

It was also necessary to have the glasses made from metal, so they wouldn't crack from the heat. To protect the actors from blistered fingers, the tumblers were filled almost to the brim with gelatin so the burning concoction would stay at the top.

On the screen, it's hilarious but when the scene was filmed on Tuesday, June 10, 1958, it was no laughing matter. Two members of the studio fire department were assigned to stand by in

Auntie Mame (Rosalind Russell, right) receives her formal introduction to Gloria Upson (Joanna Barnes, left), Patrick's (Roger Smith, center) fiancée, in the 1958 Warner Bros. film adaptation of the Broadway comedy hit *Auntie Mame*.

case the "fire water" got out of hand. And they were far from idle. During a bit of action in which Miss Russell was required to playfully slap actor Willard Waterman on the back while he held a Flaming Mame in his hand, he reacted so strongly that the contents spilled over his hand, across the dress of actress Lee Patrick who was seated beside him, and onto the floor. A potential tragedy was averted when the flames were quickly extinguished. But the casualties included a slightly blistered hand, a partially burned dress and a singed carpet.

"The Flaming Mame!" Auntie Mame (Greer Garson, right) ignites a special cocktail for her snobby in-laws-to-be, the Upsons (left to right) Doris (Dorothy Blackburn), Claude (Walter Klavun) and Gloria (Joyce Lear), in the Broadway production of *Auntie Mame.* (Courtesy of Jerome Lawrence).

In one corner of the room Mal Bert designed a 24-foot modern sculptured pylon, its base encircled by a small pond with more gold fish swimming around. In another corner was a huge Kachelofen and a wall decorated in tile imported from Italy.

The living room floor was of white ash with decorative walnut stripes and the furniture, cast in aluminum, was specially designed and built by the Warner Bros. prop department. According to the story, the unusual interior was created by famous Danish designer Yul Uhlu. In actuality, it was Warner Bros. art director Malcolm Bert, and he received an Oscar nomination for his work.

Production officially commenced on April 1, 1958, under the direction of Morton DaCosta. Fifty-six days of shooting was allotted for the principal photography with the majority of time spent on Stage #18 at the Warner Bros. studio lot.

For the Broadway stage adaptation of Patrick Dennis' novel, director DaCosta had punctuated the script with rapid pacing and highlighted the tags to each scene with blackouts, an idea he borrowed from revues and vaudeville sketches. To accomplish the blackouts on screen, DaCosta solicited the services of Warner Bros. chief electrician, Frank Flanagan, who worked out the timing on the unique fadeouts whereby only the face of star Rosalind Russell was left in view.

The stunt came to be known as the Flanagan Fade. The usual motion picture fadeout method is achieved in the film laboratory during editing of a picture where they can blur out a scene or iris-out gradually with the camera lens during shooting. The Flanagan Fade was simpler, done on the spot, as the lights were faded out with each episode break, leaving the countenance of Rosalind Russell frozen in close-up. The system not only made clear the end of a sequence, but also kept Miss Russell the center of attention for the next scene.

Henry Brandon (who played the pensive philosopher/ educator who runs an experimental, progressive school in Greenwich Village), clearly remembers the first day that he was required to be on the set. "It was the party scene where Auntie Mame traipses through one of her bright celebrations with little Patrick in tow," he says. "It was a very long and difficult scene which we spent hours lighting and setting up the camera, and it was very interesting to watch Roz prepare. She was telling me in infinite detail about the re-decorating she was going to do in the room. She *was* Mame. She was the ultimate professional."

As a young man, Brandon appeared in several of Laurel and Hardy's films, most notably 1934's *Babes in Toyland* (aka *March of the Wooden Soldiers*). He starred opposite Dame Judith Anderson in a classic stage production of *Medea* on Broadway in 1948, and gained considerable accolades. It was in this production that Tec DaCosta, at the time an actor himself, first met Brandon.

Ten years later they were reunited at a party in Malibu, California. "It was during the Christmas season of 1957," the actor recalled. "Someone at the gathering jokingly said, 'Who wants to go swimming?' It was cold outside and I guess I had to show off or something, so I said I wanted to. Three or four of us borrowed swimming trunks and ran through the party stripped to the waist. I had been working out in a gym for six or eight months and I was in the best physical shape that I had been in for years and Tec noticed that I looked rather good.

"Several months later I was called to Warner Bros. by Tec. He said he was directing *Auntie Mame* for the screen and that he was looking for someone to play the part of Acacius Paige. 'The casting department keeps sending me these body builders, none of whom can act,' he complained. I asked if there was a nude scene or something and he said no, but that he wanted someone who looks like he could have great muscles under his clothes. It wasn't an enormous part, but I was dying to be in the movie so I accepted the role," Brandon said.

Just before shooting started, Brandon asked DaCosta what the director wanted out of him for this part. Brandon remembers that DaCosta simply said, 'I want a performance. This character is sort of a pompous ass.'"

Brandon replied, "Great, I'm basing him on a ham actor who used to hang around Sardi's bar. I used to see this guy pontificating all the time with very elegant speech, which I think was covering up a Bronx accent. DaCosta said that was perfect. So that's who I was doing in the film."

Auntie Mame (Rosalind Russell, center) shares chapters of her autobiography with party guests (left to right) Gloria Upson (Joanna Barnes), Acacias Paige (Henry Brandon), Mr. Upson (Willard Waterman), Patrick (Roger Smith), Doris Upson (Lee Patrick), Mr. Babcock (Fred Clarke), Vera Charles (Coral Browne) and houseboy Ito (Yuki Shimoda), in the 1958 Warner Bros. film, *Auntie Mame*.

*

On March 24, just prior to the April 1 start of principal photography, Rosalind Russell received word that Patrick Dennis had honored her with the dedication to *Around the World With Auntie Mame*, his much-anticipated sequel to *Auntie Mame*. She immediately dashed off a telegram to his Madison Avenue apartment stating, "How can I begin to thank you for the warm and wonderful dedication. I am so touched and grateful. Know that between fittings, testing wigs and keeping Vera sober, that I love you more than ever and thank you with my whole heart."

As the principal investor in the Broadway stage production of "Auntie Mame," Russell was constantly kept apprised of how her investment was doing, even though she was no longer an acting member of the cast. On March 29, general manager Benjamin Franklin Stein wrote to her with his weekly update and stressed his concern for the continued profitability of the show. "I'm terribly worried about what the summer has in store for us," he admitted. "I don't know how long [Greer] Garson will go along with us. We have her only until May 30 and she will not give us an answer on the additional month which she has an option on. She is blaming the fact that we are taking so many people out of the show to make the movie. Naturally, this has her steamed to the sky. Yuki left last week…and the little Oliviere boy is adequate enough to keep going but finding a boy [to play Patrick] is hard. Thank goodness Peggy Cass doesn't have to go until the beginning of May. This is the best news I could have gotten from Hollywood."

*

On the final day of filming at Warner Bros. there was the customary wrap party on the set. For gifts they presented their star with such gags as a jeweled cigarette holder, a pressure cooker, a sales book, a silver goblet, a Siamese bracelet and a small pocket mirror. Rosalind's friend Cris Alexander, who had a shining moment in the film portraying Mr. Loomis, the bombastic floor manager at Macy's department store who fires Mame Dennis, remembers a harbinger of things to come. Alexander recalls that Lucille Ball showed up at the celebration. "I just happened to be standing with Rosalind at the moment when Lucy came along. Mind you, this was 1958 and though it's common knowledge that she was rather a bundle of wrinkles [without stage make up. adhesive surgical tape lifts and temporary "skyhook" face lift devices], I remember I was absolutely shocked to see her close up. She was more wrinkled than anybody I have ever seen. She said, 'Rosalind, you're the only person I have ever been jealous of. If there was one part I would give my soul to do, it's this one.'"

*

Warner Bros. previewed *Auntie Mame* in Westwood, California, just prior to its release, and the response was phenomenally enthusiastic. Audience-reaction screenings are an important part of testing motion pictures for last minute adjustments or fine-tuning a film for a specific target audience. *Auntie Mame* could not be improved.

Henry Brandon remembers there was a sneak preview to which no one in the film was invited. However, he was tipped off by a friend that *Auntie Mame* would be screened for a recruited audience in Westwood. With the help of a friend in the sound department, Brandon managed to gain entrance to the secret screening.

"I would not advise filmmakers to preview a picture in

Westwood unless they want a very intelligent audience reaction," Brandon later said. "Those UCLA kids (Westwood is at the edge of the UCLA campus) laughed through every word of my dialogue, because they were watching two ladies in the corner of the screen! I never noticed while we were shooting, but in that corner of the film frame, just off to my left elbow, were two lesbian ladies. Their purses didn't have lipstick or powder, it was chains and wrenches and steam hammers. I've seen the film four or five times since with an audience and nobody notices them, just those sharp kids from UCLA."

Inclued at this preview was the hilarious scene written by Comden & Green in which Mame – during her series of attempts to hold a job – tried selling pressure-cookers door-to-door. The payoff of this episode finds Mame demonstrating the apparatus at a farmhouse, and of course calamitous disaster when the pressure-cooker explodes blowing a hole in the house. As the sequence ends, Mame was seen climing out through the hole and dashing up a country road.

That hilarious scene, however, was a casualty of the film's length, and was ultimately left on the cutting room floor.

For months prior to the December release, the Warner Bros. publicity machine had been churning out exploitation ideas to ensure that this highly anticipated project would be all that the studio knew it could be. The publicists in the promotions department suggested such quirky marketing gimmicks as giving away long cigarette holders like those used in the film to the first woman attending each theatre. They recommended that a special cocktail called The Flaming Mame be created at local clubs with appropriate cards at each table with such written copy as: "Auntie Mame suggests you try this..."

At theatres showing *Auntie Mame* there were recordings with a special message in a theatrical voice announcing, "This is

In a scene cut from the 1958 Warner Bros. film *Auntie Mame,* Mame (Rosalind Russell) is forced to take on a series of odd and disastrous jobs, including pressure cooker sales person.

your Auntie Mame. I'll be looking for you at..." with the show times announced.

The ads and posters proclaimed: "All the joy in the world for all the world to enjoy!"

"You haven't really laughed until you've seen *Auntie Mame* on the screen!"

"This year everybody's spending Christmas with Auntie Mame!"

"They're all here. That mad, marvelous Auntie Mame mob!"

Finally, *Auntie Mame* had its world premiere engagement at Radio City Music Hall in New York, December 4. A star-studded list of celebrities was in attendance as the house lights dimmed and the overture began.

Opening titles of motion pictures have long been uninspired. They usually have consisted of Leo's roaring face, Paramount's icy summit, Columbia's dimestore Statue of Miss Liberty or other trademarks followed by star billing, cast of characters and the names of everybody else whose contracts demand mention. Sometimes an atmospheric matframe or suggestive cartoon work has adorned the listings, but the credits for *Auntie Mame* were unique and interesting.

As the stirring Bronislau Kaper score begins with the music to "Drifting" ("Auntie Mame's Theme"), the red-gloved hand of Rosalind Russell comes into close-up holding a kaleidoscope – that gayest of toys. The velvet covered tube is turned toward the camera which comes in for a close-up of the multicolored prisms inside the tube. As the colors blend and separate, the little glass jewels spell out "Auntie Mame" and the film's credits. The West Coast premiere was held at Grauman's Chinese Theatre on Christmas Night 1958.

On February 19, 1959, Rosalind Russell continued a long Hollywood tradition when she inscribed her name in wet cement in the forecourt of the world famous theatre on Hollywood Boulevard. In a brief ceremony that began at 7:15 p.m., just prior to the start of the evening's first performance of *Auntie Mame*, Russell impressed her shoes and hands into the gray, mucky compound, continuing a tradition that began in 1927 when Sid Grauman happened to notice that Mary Pickford had accidentally stepped into wet cement in front of his theatre. Grauman had been conducting a tour of his theatre for Pickford, Douglas Fairbanks and Norma Talmadge prior to its opening. The gracious host made light of the faux pas and immediately invited Fairbanks and Talmadge to add their footprints

Hollywood's famed Chinese Theatre played host to the exclusive opening engagement of Warner Bros. *Auntie Mame* in 1958 (Author's collection)

for posterity. Miss Russell's ritual was the first since Rock Hudson and Elizabeth Taylor were recognized two years earlier, during the theatrical run of *Giant*.

*

When the 1958 Academy Award nominations were announced in March 1959, *Auntie Mame* was mentioned in six categories including best picture. However, as the highest-grossing ($9 million) and one of the most critically acclaimed films of the year, one nomination was conspicuously missing – director Morton DaCosta.

"I think it's interesting that *Auntie Mame* and my later film, *The Music Man* earned 17 Academy Award nominations between them, but I was never nominated. I've never even been nominated for the Tony Award, despite having some of the biggest grossing and critically acclaimed hits of all time on Broadway. I consider this rather an oddity," DaCosta observed.

If there had been a People's Choice Award in 1959, Rosalind Russell would have won best actress honors, hands down. But the voters for Oscar are seldom in sync with the tastes of the general public. According to a survey taken on the eve of the Academy Awards ceremony in 1959, Susan Hayward, Hollywood's ultimate choice for best actress over Rosalind Russell that year, received no better than third place when the public was consulted. The survey was taken by Sindlinger and Company, analysts who had frequently performed survey's for the movie industry in attempting to predict trends and public tastes. Their report also revealed that *Auntie Mame* was attended by more Americans over twelve years of age during 1959 than any other motion picture.

Though Russell and Spencer Tracy were the odds-on

favorites to walk away with the Oscar, neither won their category that year.

"Comedies seldom win," Russell said after the awards ceremony, "and besides, Susan [Hayward, Best Actress winner] was excellent. Next year I gotta try a gas chamber with all those crazy pellets," she quipped referring to Hayward's highly charged portrayal of an alleged murderess who meets her death by execution in *I Want To Live.*

Ingrid Bergman was so incensed by the Oscar snub, she announced that if Russell couldn't have won for her tour-de-force performance, then the Motion Picture Academy should have given her a special Oscar.

Mame Dennis (Rosalind Russell, left) is shocked to meet Beauregard's (Forrest Tucker, second from right) Southern family, including flatulent matriarch Mrs. Burnside (Carol Veazie, center) and gold-digging cousin Sally Cato MacDougal in the 1958 Warner Bros. film *Auntie Mame.*

Auntie Mame (Rosalind Russell) faces a bleak Depression-era Christmas, but is comforted by her nephew Patrick (Jan Handzlik), in Warner Bros. 1958 comedy, *Auntie Mame.*

As trustee for the Knickerbocker Bank, Dwight Babcock (Fred Clarke, center) rules that Auntie Mame (Rosalind Russell, left) must send young Patrick (Jan Handzlik, right) off to boarding school, in Warner Bros. 1958 comedy, *Auntie Mame.*
©1958 Warner Bros. Pictures, Inc. Renewed 1986. All Rights Reserved.

After losing her fortune in the stock market crash, Auntie Mame (Rosalind Russell) is comforted at Christmastime by her faithful servant Norah Muldoon (Connie Gilchrist) in the 1958 Warner Bros. comedy, *Auntie Mame.*
©1958 Warner Bros. Pictures, Inc. Renewed 1986. All Rights Reserved.

Auntie Mame (Rosalind Russell, center) pays a visit to "Upson Downs" the home of nephew Patrick's future in-laws Claude Upson (Willard Waterman, left) and Doris (Lee Patrick, right), in the Warner Bros. comedy, *Auntie Mame.*
©1958 Warner Bros. Pictures, Inc. Renewed 1986. All Rights Reserved.

Fred Clarke starred as the Babbitt-like banker Mr. Babcock opposite Rosalind Russell in Warner Bros. 1958 comedy, *Auntie Mame.*
©1958 Warner Bros. Pictures, Inc. Renewed 1986. All Rights Reserved.

CHAPTER SIX

Mame: The Broadway Musical

THEY CALLED IT *AUNTIE MONEY.*

After two best-selling novels, a smash Broadway play and box office triumph in Hollywood, the Auntie Mame character continued to be a touchstone for success, a bottomless gold mine that harvested years of royalties for author Patrick Dennis, producers Robert Fryer and Lawrence Carr, playwrights Lawrence and Lee, and Rosalind Russell.

Few theatrical properties to this day have the wide appeal of *Auntie Mame,* and when the amateur rights were made available, stock companies and school drama departments created innumerable productions worldwide. School groups loved to mount this play because the cast of players was large and thus capable of supporting an above average number of student thespians. Stock companies adopted it for their repertoire because it seemed that no matter who portrayed the madcap title character, every production was a sure-fire hit and audience charmer.

From the very beginning of the play's genesis in 1955, there had been discussions about turning the property into a musical. Meetings were held among the producers, playwrights and backers to discuss the idea, but nothing developed out of these talks until 1964 when Broadway producer Joe Harris and wife, Sylvia, joined forces with Fryer and Carr to form the producing firm of Fryer, Carr and Harris. Among the New York stage productions that the Harrises had produced were *Tovarich* and *Make a Million.*

Robert Fryer said of the new business union at the time, "Of course creative people should dominate the theatre, but we feel strongly that the theatre should be run on a businesslike basis."

The four-member board of directors of this new entertainment concern were Joe Harris as chairman of the board, Lawrence Carr as president, Robert Fryer, as vice president, and Sylvia Harris as secretary-treasurer. It was determined that every decision must be unanimous before a new project would be produced, and the group agreed that their first priority would be to bring Gwen Verdon back to Broadway.

In addition to seeking a project for Verdon and also Fryer and Carr's stage pet Shirley Booth, it took very little deliberation to decide to immediately start work on producing a musical version of *Auntie Mame* to be based on the original character but not necessarily on the successful comedy of 1956.

Robert Fryer remembers that after the success of the second Auntie Mame novel, *Around the World With Auntie Mame* by Patrick Dennis, and the Warner Bros. film adaptation of *Auntie Mame* with Rosalind Russell, Jimmy Carr brought up the subject of checking into when their rights for making *Auntie Mame* into a musical would lapse.

"It was almost a fluke," Fryer remembers. "We got out the old contract and found that we had only two days left on our option." In 48 hours the rights would have reverted back to Lawrence and Lee, the play's original authors.

The producers called agent Annie Laurie Williams and were reminded that Lawrence and Lee had stipulated in their original 1955 agreement that if a musical based on their play was ever made, that they would be the ones to write the book.

On August 3, 1964, contracts were signed between Fryer, Carr, Harris and Patrick Dennis to option the rights to make a musical out of his "Auntie Mame" property. Dennis received an advance of $500, with the agreement that the producers would pay him an additional $500 every six months until the play was produced or abandoned. Moreover, it was further expressed that if Fryer, Carr and Harris did abandon the project at any time before production, that Lawrence and Lee would have one year from the date the producers dropped the project to find another producer.

"The thing to remember," said Charles Adams Baker, who was an agent with the William Morris Agency, and who represented several of the actors in the eventual show, "was that the project at that time was not considered a feather in anyone's cap. It was much too soon on the heels of the 'freak' success of the play, which was certainly considered Roz Russell's turf; somewhat as if I came to you with the staggering idea of doing a musical version of *Lettice & Lovage* – *without* Maggie Smith!"

With hindsight, and knowing now what a hit the musical show ultimately turned out to be, one would think that the producers would have had a relatively easy task convincing potential backers to invest in another incarnation of the madcap Mame. But this was definitely not the case with the musical version of *Auntie Mame* .

John Bowab, the associate producer of the musical, recalls, "The problem was that potential backers thought it was a revival of the comedy play. Many people said, 'I saw it with Rosalind Russell; it was a musical then.'

"Tec DaCosta had directed the original play in a musical form," Bowab said. "When I would call potential backers, including some of the original investors, they would insist that I meant this was a revival. I would have to explain that it was a new musical, and they would invariable ask, 'What happened to the one by Lawrence and Lee?' It was very confusing at the time and strange to do a musical so close to the end of the run of the straight play upon which it was based."

The name Jerry Herman eventually played a momentous role in procuring the necessary funds to back this new theatrical venture. Herman's Tony Award-winning score for *Hello, Dolly!* starring Carol Channing had been an enormous smash hit on Broadway. That production won ten Tony Awards and played at the St. James Theatre for a remarkable 2,844 performances. As the composer now says, "I was feeling no pain."

Herman recalls that his relationship with the Auntie Mame character really began when he was a young man. "I read the book and I remember laughing out loud. It's very hard to read a book and make noise but I screamed with laughter. Then I saw the Rosalind Russell play and had the overwhelming joy of being introduced to the character in the flesh. I had no idea that I would ever have anything personal to do with Auntie Mame."

Herman graduated from the University of Miami in 1954 and returned to the city of his birth, New York, to begin what has become a legendary career in the theatre. Having written a successful revue in college, Herman opened his first professional show *I Feel Wonderful* at the Theater De Lys in New York on October 18, 1954.

Though that production ran for only 49 performances, Herman was encouraged to continue writing. But it was six years before another Jerry

Tony Award winner Jerry Herman composed the classic songs for *Mame*. (Author's collection)

Herman musical made its way to the well hewn boards of a New York theater. That show, *Parade*, which Herman also directed, opened at the MacDougal Street Theatre on January 20, 1960, and played for 95 performances.

According to *Daily Variety*, the most important footnote to *Parade* is the fact that producer Gerard Oestreicher saw the show, was impressed with the composer/lyricist's ability to write upbeat, hummable songs, and signed Herman to write the score for *Milk and Honey*. That show became Jerry Herman's first major hit, opening at the Martin Beck Theatre October 10, 1961. *Milk and Honey* gave Herman his first Tony Award nomination and played for 543 performances.

Herman's next musical, *Madame Aphrodite*, was less favorably received. It opened off-Broadway at the Orpheum on December 29, 1961, and closed 13 performances later. Still, the word was out that Jerry Herman was the musical theatre's most important new find, and he was signed to write the score for *Hello, Dolly!*, the musical version of Thornton Wilder's *The Matchmaker*.

Nineteen sixty-four was an auspicious year for the young composer. That year, his memorable words and music for *Hello, Dolly!* garnered the songwriter his first Tony Award as best composer and lyricist, his first Grammy Award for the title song, and first gold record – also for the title song. Then, he contemplated his next step.

It was autumn. Herman recalls that he received a telephone call from Jerome Lawrence asking if the composer would care to meet and have lunch with him and his partner, Robert E. Lee. The trio agreed to rendezvous at Sardi's, Broadway's legendary theatre crowd eatery.

Considered the musical theatre's newest *wunderkind*, Herman was in great demand by virtually every producer in town, who wanted him to write the score for new shows. His rivals disparaged Herman, saying he had an infuriatingly simple skill, not unlike that of Irving Berlin.

In addition to being one of the most respected talents on Broadway, Jerry Herman is an optimistic and enthusiastic human being. He was of course familiar with the work of Lawrence and Lee and genuinely delighted that these two distinguished, highly accomplished, talents wanted to meet him. He was equally anxious to meet them.

Though Herman wasn't sure how to recognize the playwrights, within seconds of entering Sardi's it was apparent that they were each looking for somebody. The men introduced themselves, shook hands and were ushered to a table. For the first few minutes they all made small talk and offered praise for each others' work.

"It was the middle of the day and it was very quiet in the half-empty restaurant," recalls Herman. "Then, after about three minutes Jerry Lawrence turned to me in his affable voice and said, 'How would you like to make a musical out of *Auntie Mame?*'

"I just yelled out something guttural. I think I said, 'Wow!' or 'Oh, my God!' I made an uncharacteristic [for me] kind of noise. I'm a very quiet man, and I know that many people turned around to see what was happening in my direction. I really made a kind of uproar in that restaurant. I laugh about it today because I think it's the only scene I ever made in public. But it was so apt, so correct," he says. "I knew it was right. The idea clicked and I knew I could write something that I could be happy with as an offspring."

Herman was Lawrence & Lee's logical choice as a collaborator because of his tuneful treatment of two other celebrated ladies, Clara Weiss of *Milk and Honey* and Dolly Levi of *Hello, Dolly!* And Lawrence and Lee weren't exactly strangers to the world of musical comedy. While best-known to the public for non-musical works, their first Broadway venture, after years of creating miniature musicals for radio's *Railroad Hour* program, was the 1948 hit *Look, Ma, I'm Dancin'*.

Within minutes, the illustrious triumvirate agreed to a collaboration that would prove to be one of the most successful in musical theatre history.

*

When it was formally announced that Jerry Herman had signed with Fryer, Carr and Harris to compose the score for their new musical based on Lawrence and Lee's book, some cynics felt that he was an odd choice for this particular project. Their negative attitude stemmed from the fact that Herman was not considered a sophisticated writer. He was a popular writer, but when one thought of who should write an *Mame* score, one might first think of someone like Cole Porter, a composer renowned for his wit and sophistication.

In the 1960s however, Porter was seriousl ill and virtually retired and a reculse. He died on October 15, 1964.

Hiring Jerry Herman proved to be one of the smartest moves the producers could have made toward the fruition of this project. Herman's songs ultimately brought a warm and human quality to the Mame Dennis character.

"Wit, sophistication and bitchiness would have been all wrong for this show," John Bowab says knowingly. "Jerry Herman's music is very tender and it went right to the human side of the Mame character. His music heightened the sensitivity between little Patrick and his outrageous aunt."

It was really unfair and premature for Herman's detractors to judge his music as unsophisticated. He wrote some very sophisticated songs for his previous Broadway hits including "Shalom" and "There's No Reason in the World" from *Milk and Honey* and "It Only Takes a Moment" from *Hello, Dolly!*, among others.

As with any creative endeavor, there are countless artistic and technical variables that lead to the success or failure of a Broadway show. It's difficult now to see how this production of *Mame* could have missed being a hit, but, indeed, considering several of the original concepts and early obstacles, it could very well have been a disappointing mess.

Focus now turned to seeing their musicalized *Mame*. When pre-production on the show began in 1964, producer Sylvia Harris announced, "We tied down a very big star for the role the other day. We won't say who it is until August, but the show will have a brand new title ("My Best Girl") and a brand new look."

The star Mrs. Harris was referring to turned out to be Broadway legend Mary Martin, who had been approached by the producers and convinced that *Mame* would be the perfect vehicle for her triumphant return to the Broadway stage. And she appeared to love the notion of portraying what had already become one of the theatre's great characters.

The star of *Leave It to Me, One Touch of Venus, South Pacific, Peter Pan, The Sound of Music,* Martin was a magical name that the producers knew would draw investors and audiences alike. Her flops were few and her hits were legendary. Martin's only concern – at least verbally – was with the show's musical score, which had yet to be completely written when she showed interest in doing the role. A clause in her preliminary agreement provided that she could withdraw from the project if she found the musical material unacceptable for any reason.

At the birth of *Mame*, the creative minds were determined that it was not going to be just *Auntie Mame* with music. It was to be a brand new show with only the bare bones of the original story intact and tailored to conform to Mary Martin's personality. "We conceived '*Mame* as a new work and tried to tell it as lyrically and joyfully as possible with music," Jerome Lawrence said.

For instance, Martin had a southern accent, and writers Lawrence and Lee decided that if the story-line took her to Georgia with her fiancé, Beauregard, as in the original Rosalind Russell escapade, the humor would have less impact. As Lawrence and Lee revealed, "In an early version of the musical, long before rehearsals began, we experimented with the idea of sending Mame to the British horsey countryside instead of to Peckerwood in the American South. Her 'Bo' (for "Bolingbroke," not "Beauregard") was an English Lord, who made her the 'Duchess of Burnside."

They felt it would be funnier to have Mame go to London to meet his aristocratic family rather than to an ante-bellum Southern plantation as in the original story. Also, they wanted to give Beauregard a stutter.

Soon however, the idea of turning Beau into an English Lord was scrapped, and one of the brightest of Jerry Herman's songs, "Mame The Most!" had to be thrown out. (It was replaced by the title song, "Mame.") Billionaire Aristotle Onassis was in the news at the time, and another concept for the show was to have Mame marry a Greek shipping magnate much like Onassis. Early script ideas suggested that a civil war break out in Greece, and Mame, bearing her infinite diplomacy, would go up into the mountains and bring the warring factions back down together in peace.

Still another draft of the musical opened with Mame on a giant bed surrounded by portraits of all the adoring men in her life. In a hoped for rousing musical opening, the paintings would spring to life, their subjects singing the praises of Mame, extolling her infinite virtues. According to theatre historian John Fricke, "Mame in bed, surrounded by portraits of the men in her life, was an idea uncomfortably close to the one-woman-surrounded-by-seven-men scripting of the 1962 musical *Little Me* (also based on a book by Patrick Dennis). All seven men in *Little Me* were played by Sid Caesar."

"When people say now that this show couldn't have missed, with so many changes it very well could have been a *disaster*," says Bowab.

By the time *Mame* was ready for pre-production, the producers had been involved in many award-winning and hit Broadway shows. They knew their way around the theatre and surrounded themselves with only the very best talent in the industry. For *Mame,* they gathered a coterie of technical and creative talent with many major hits between them.

Auntie Mame's original director, Morton DaCosta, remembers that he was asked to do the musical but that by this time he'd had enough of the character. "I was worn out with it," DaCosta remembered. "I told the producers they should get another person for a different point of view. But had I known that it was going to end up like the play I did, with songs stuck in, I would have said thank you very much and taken the money and run. Apparently they tried to change it drastically and it just didn't work. So they went back to what did work. It seems that my original work was the definitive one for the property."

Director Joshua Logan and choreographer Onna White were among the first to be assigned to the challenge of bringing this show to fruition. However, before long it became apparent that Logan was not going to be the appropriate director to launch this new musical. His vision for the show included casting Nanette Fabray in the lead, a notion that none of the other producers found acceptable.

"Josh Logan wanted major changes in the story, which we felt would disappoint all the people who loved this character," Jerry Herman says. "There were artistic differences and we ultimately only worked together for a few weeks."

A mercurial talent, Logan was infamous for totally reconstructing material that had been completely acceptable to him the day before. Onna White, one of the most celebrated choreographers in Broadway history, remembers that this was her biggest apprehension about working with Logan. She recalls, "I went to Jimmy Carr and said, 'You know I love Josh, but I'm not thrilled about working with him.'"

Carr asked if she had any better ideas for a director. Indeed she had. "I just finished doing a show [Half a Sixpence] with Gene Saks," she said. "He's extremely bright and easy to work with."

Before becoming one of the theatre's most renowned directors, Saks was an actor of note, appearing in such stage productions as *A Shot in the Dark, The Tenth Man, Middle of the Night* and as Charles the Chipmunk in both the stage and screen productions of *A Thousand Clowns.* Saks then moved into directing at the urging of his wife, actress Beatrice Arthur.

"I pushed him into it," Arthur said in an interview. "I was aware, long before Gene was, of his ability to work with actors where so-called directors couldn't."

Saks was in Boston directing *Generation* starring Henry Fonda when Onna White contacted him and asked if he'd be interested in doing another musical with her.

"What is it?" he inquired.

"*Auntie Mame,*" she said.

As many others before had asked, Saks queried, "Wasn't that already done as a musical?"

He ultimately agreed to come back to New York to discuss the project.

Once Gene Saks committed to direct *Mame*, Robert Fryer and composer Jerry Herman boarded a plane for the long flight to Brazil to meet once again with Mary Martin for whom they would unveil the new musical score.

"She lived in the jungles of Brazil," remembers Jerry Herman, "and we had to take a tiny plane from Rio de Janeiro to an even smaller South American city. Then we boarded a jeep with a driver who took us through a very rough and frightening countryside."

Upon arrival at the Mary Martin-Richard Halliday hacienda, where the tenants raised bananas, avocados, mangos and pineapples, the two men from Manhattan were greeted warmly by the reigning monarch of Broadway and her husband. "She was a grand hostess, and we had a wonderful time with her," Herman recalls.

But after playing the score for their leading lady, the producer and composer received the shock of their respective careers – Martin turned the project down flat.

"I played her the songs I had written up to that moment and she was very enthusiastic. She was a warm and terrific lady. But when it came time to sign a contract, for some personal reasons, she declined to do the show."

Herman believes that Martin perhaps felt as Ethel Merman had when approached to play Dolly Levi several years earlier— she had turned to them and said, "I don't even want to hear the score because I am tired of living my life in dressing rooms." "I think that moment might have come to Mary, who up to that moment had literally been on stage all her adult life," Herman says.

Martin used the excuse that the score failed to captivate her, even though the music that Herman played that day was almost exactly the music that has become a Broadway standard.

"It changed very little from the time they met with Martin until opening night at the Winter Garden Theatre in New York," John Bowab says. "The feeling was that Miss Martin simply didn't want to play the part and thus exercised her option based on the score.

"I think it was shock," Bowab continues about the incident. "Nothing changed dramatically in the score, especially Mame's numbers. The rousing song 'It's Today,' was always there, with slight lyric modifications. Part of the lyric had been 'Pass the peanuts...' I remember Jimmy Carr saying that Mame would never say, 'Pass the peanuts.' So Jerry changed it to 'light the candles, get the ice out...'"

"It was very similar to when I counted on Ethel Merman for *Hello, Dolly!* and had her in mind when I wrote a lot of the songs, and then was told she wouldn't do it," says Herman.

Confounded, the search began in earnest for a new star. The financing had been set, the Winter Garden Theatre had been booked and Gene Saks was ready to direct the show. "We had to find somebody, even if it meant taking a lady off 44th Street and just putting a costume on her!" Herman says, only half joking.

Once the news began to travel along the short Broadway grapevine that Mary Martin had turned down the part, it seemed that every actress who ever trod the boards was on the phone to their respective agents begging to be considered for the role.

The list of stars who were asked to audition but who were not interested was a very short one. Ethel Merman topped that column, followed closely by Gwen Verdon. Though nobody really thought either was right for the part, they were both considered major names in the theatre. Verdon, who had previously starred in the musical *Redhead* for Fryer and Carr, fortuitously turned down the producers' offer to do *Mame* and that same season she created one of the greatest triumphs of her career as Charity Hope Valentine in *Sweet Charity* (also a Fryer, Carr & Harris production).

"It seemed that half the world wanted the part of Mame," says Bowab, "and the other half was afraid of competing with the legend that Rosalind Russell established for the part."

It was different for a show with a reputation like *Hello, Dolly!* As strong an impact as Ruth Gordon made in the original play, *The Matchmaker*, or Shirley Booth in the film version, the character of Dolly was never a monumental folklore heroine as Auntie Mame had become. People would say, "Oh, she's an Auntie Mame," but they wouldn't say, "My aunt was Dolly."

"We ultimately brought in every known musical comedy lady of the day, but none of them hit all the right marks," says Jerry Herman. "Mame is really a very difficult role to play; it's deceptive because it's such fun to do. Everyone thinks that just anybody can step into that part and be wonderful in it."

One of the major aspects of the character that changed because of Jerry Herman's score for Mary Martin was her strident persona. Stars such as Elaine Stitch would have been a logical choice during the early stages of pre-production, but by the time the musical score was finished it was no longer necessary for the character to be caustic or rough. The quality that was missing in most of the people who wanted the part was great personal warmth, which Herman's music would embellish.

"First of all, the part requires a real lady," says Herman. "The more elegant the lady, the more successful she will be as Mame. But underneath she also has to have some wild, unpredictable humor. That juxtaposition is not easy to find."

Over the next several months, the director, producers and writers saw practically every leading lady in show business. The long list of stars they deliberated over included Eve Arden, Lauren Bacall, Lucille Ball, Kaye Ballard, Constance Bennett,

Georgia Brown, Kitty Carlisle, Barbara Cook, Bette Davis, Doris Day, Olivia de Havilland, Phyllis Diller, Irene Dunne, Arlene Francis, Mitzi Gaynor, Dolores Gray, Katharine Hepburn, Lena Horne, Dinah Shore, Simone Signoret and Elaine Stritch.

But something was missing from each one. Either they were superb actresses but didn't have the right vocal equipment, or had great show voices but were missing some other element. No one actress seemed to have the exact combination of qualities that were crucial for the role.

Jerome Lawrence remembers that one of his Malibu, California neighbors and friends was Angela Lansbury. "She lived down the road and I went to her one day and said that I wanted to pitch her for the role, and would she be interested.

"'Damn right!'" she replied.

"I took her to lunch and we talked about it. Then I called Jerry Herman in New York, who agreed that Angela would be wonderful. 'She'd be perfect,' he said. Let me go get a program and I'll handle it.'"

Jerry Herman was living on 9th Street in Greenwich Village at the time and he remembers that after searching for a star for some time and then getting Jerome Lawrence's call, he began going through his vast collection of *Playbills*, those programs of "Who's in the Cast" which are given out at every Broadway performance. After pouring over these theatre magazines, he came across a *Playbill* from the Stephen Sondheim musical *Anyone Can Whistle*, starring Angela Lansbury.

"That show had only run on Broadway for a week but I had been fortunate enough to see it," Herman remembers. "I suddenly got that feeling...the hair stood up on my arms. I quickly got on the phone and I called Jimmy Carr and said, 'I think I have somebody that I would love you to see. Her name is Angela Lansbury.'"

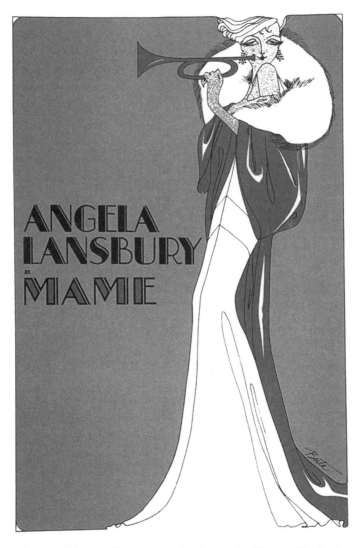

The world-famous Berta poster for the musical *Mame*. (Author's collection).

"Oh, she's a marvelous actress," Carr agreed, "but I don't think she sings well enough and I don't think she's a musical comedy lady at all!"

But Herman was adamant, "I saw her in *Anyone Can Whistle*. She belted out one song after another and was superb in that production. She has a musical background, and for God's sake, let's see her!"

The producer was totally unswayed by Herman's excitement, and the seemingly absurd notion of seeing this Lansbury woman was dismissed point blank. For one thing, Carr didn't feel that the three-time Academy Award nominee was a big enough name for his show.

Herman endured a week of acute frustration. All he could think of was Angela as Mame. Finally, he confronted Robert Fryer.

"I have never asked you for anything on this show," Herman stated. "I've been a good sport and just done my work. This is the first time I'm asking for a favor. I would like you to fly Angela Lansbury out to audition for *Mame*. You've flown all these other people from all around the world – you even flew me to Brazil. You can certainly send for Angela Lansbury!"

The producers finally acquiesced, purely it seems, to pacify Herman. They still weren't any more interested in Lansbury than when Carr first dismissed the idea. Forced to make all the arrangements himself, Herman called Lansbury in California, and invited her to come to Manhattan. "We'll go to lunch and talk," he said to her.

Herman clearly remembers the day he met with Angela Lansbury: "The bell rang in my apartment and this stunning woman was standing there. We had an absolutely delightful lunch at Longchamps on Fifth Avenue. It was spring, and I remember that at the end of lunch I turned to her and did something so terrible, so wrong. I said, 'You have to have this part!

You're going to think I'm bananas. But my instincts are so strong that you will be absolutely smashing!'"

To insure a great response at the next day's audition, Herman asked Lansbury if she would mind learning two of the songs from the show that afternoon. "If they hear you sing these songs, they will absolutely flip out," Herman promised. "Every other lady who has come in has sung her own material. But nobody knows these songs."

Lansbury happily agreed and also enjoyed the little intrigue. "So I spent the afternoon with her. She learned 'It's Today' and 'If He Walked Into My Life.'"

Herman promised that "by hook or by crook" when it was Lansbury's turn to audition he would be in the orchestra pit to play the piano for her. "I'll do an intro and you just walk on," he instructed.

The following day the producers, composer, playwrights, director and choreographer all gathered at the empty Winter Garden Theatre. Herman confided to the assemblage that he had met with Lansbury the previous day and was very impressed with her. "I said no more," Herman remembers. "But about three minutes later I excused myself, as if I were going to the men's room. I found my way down to the orchestra pit, climbed in and the stage manager announced: 'Gentlemen – Angela Lansbury.'"

An elegant and confident Lansbury walked out from the stage wings, took her place upstage center and with a big musical flourish from Jerry Herman at the keyboard below, she belted out the lyrics: "Light the candles, get the ice out...," from the now classic tune, "It's Today."

As John Hallowell wrote in his June 17, 1966 cover story for *Life* magazine, "Many of the established stars who were hot for the part had resorted to the time-honored gambit of refusing the 'insult' of an audition. But Angela, by the very grace with which she agreed to try out, turned the trick of making the others look like pompous amateurs.

"Not, however, that the audition was anything but an ordeal." Hallowell reported in his article: "'Out there in the house sat all those important figures,'" she [Lansbury] recalls. "'At least I had Jerry Herman at the piano. And the two songs he'd taught me. So I sang. In the middle Mr. Logan said, "I can't see your face,"' Angela stopped with a look of terror.

Angela Lansbury became the toast of Broadway with her Tony Award-winning role as Mame Dennis in the musical *Mame*. (Courtesy of Jerome Lawrence).

"'Mr. Logan asked somebody with the work light to mask it with a script and point it right at me. It was a damn good thing I was used to movies, with all those lights in my face. I started again. Mr. Logan stopped me, 'I still can't see you.' So up they all come on stage, right up for a good close *look*, for God's sake. It was summer, all very hot, and they were holding raincoats and wearing dark glasses – a regular lineup. I did the songs again. Then they said 'goodbye,' 'thank you.' that was all."

Lansbury flew home to California feeling the trip had been a waste of her time.

Jerry Herman remembers things a bit differently, that the small audience nearly fell out of their respective velour-covered seats when Lansbury performed. They had never heard the songs sung so well – and not by anyone other than Herman. He recalls that when Lansbury finished the first song, she quietly walked over to the side of the stage and did the powerfully poignant "If He Walked Into My Life."

Herman remembers that with Lansbury's infectious British warmth, it was apparent that she was one of the few actresses who exuded the spirit necessary to carry this show. The audition was sensational, he said. The small coterie of theatrical know-it-all's were stunned by this revelation. All agreed that Lansbury was a great discovery.

But, unbelievably, for all her abilities and the "great personal warmth" the producers had said they were looking for, Lansbury was still the dark horse on the list of people being considered for *Mame*.

Lansbury's agent, Charles Adams Baker, recalls, "Angela surely was a brave and confident girl. But her position on Broadway was somewhat similar to what she enjoyed in films …everybody's favorite co-worker, but not a 'ticket seller.' But she sensed that *Mame* was her brass ring and she went for it. Not by trying to knock anyone else out, but by hard work, infinite patience, and just raw talent."

"The thing I remember most about her first audition is how strong her personality was," recalls Bowab. "We expected a strong lady but Angela had such pizzazz. But it was ultimately disappointing because she didn't seem to have the vocal range for the score. I also remember that the stage lighting was terrible. They had not paid to put the lights on in the theatre so we were using only a work light and it made Angela looked heavier, possibly 20 pounds or more than when she eventually played the part."

Lansbury wanted this role as much or more as she had ever wanted anything else in her career. She returned to California after the audition and began studying with a vocal coach who helped her add three notes at the top and bottom of her singing range. She was determined that she would be at least seriously considered for the role of Mame. She ultimately auditioned four times, flying back and forth from California to New York – at her own expense.

"I went out and bought six red rosebushes and planted them" she said in the Hallowell *Life* magazine story, to distract herself from the agony of waiting to hear the outcome of her auditions. "I don't cover my disappointments. You can't do that – I just clear them out," she said.

"In the evenings," Hallowell's article continues, "after taking long walks on the beach, she would wait with her family, jumping like a porpoise when the phone rang. 'There we'd be, scared together, for bloomin' months. Anthony coming in with surfboards and sand and dogs and cats and me by that goddam phone...'"

In the meantime, other candidates were still being seen and auditioned for the prestigious role including Lauren Bacall, Tammy Grimes, Shirl Conway, Georgia Brown, Kaye Ballard, Geraldine Page and Beatrice Arthur, the director's wife. It was very strongly rumored in the columns in late 1965 that Ann Sothern had been cast as Mame, at which point the show's working title was *My Best Girl.*

Jimmy Carr had insisted from the beginning that whomever they chose, that person had to be news in the theatre. Any of those stars would have fit the bill, perhaps most notably Geraldine Page, and an audition was scheduled for the star of *Sweet Bird of Youth* and *Summer and Smoke*, at the producers' offices at 445 Park Avenue. It turned out to be a disaster. The audition was kept a secret because Page had already been signed to do a musical for Jule Styne (which ultimately never materialized).

Bowab remembers that Page entered the 30-seat theatre in

their office dressed to the nines. "She looked like a star. However, she became extremely nervous and sang badly. It broke our hearts because Page was a beloved and respected artist in the theatre. Her placement in the show would have been the *news* that Carr insisted upon."

After the producers had exhausted their list of actresses, Jerry Herman and Jerome Lawrence, who had loyally been championing Angela Lansbury all along, finally forced the issue of Lansbury's participation. The two main obstacles to her being cast in the show – Mary Martin and Josh Logan – were now history, and Herman and Lawrence remained resolute that Lansbury would be the big news that Carr wanted.

A quirky little incident that would prove to be a harbinger of things to come occurred the previous year, the day after Bowab and Carr attended the closing night performance of *Anyone Can Whistle*. As fate would have it, they were driving with agent Gus Schirmer down Beekman Place in New York. As they rounded the corner at 50th Street, Angela and her husband, Peter Shaw, were coming up from Central Park. Angela Lansbury...Beekman Place...Auntie Mame. Bowab took this as an omen and didn't forget about the star all during the long and difficult casting process.

It's difficult for Broadway and TV fans of today to accept, but Angela Lansbury was not considered a bankable star when she auditioned for *Mame*. She was a respected actress in Hollywood but had completed only one previous Broadway musical-comedy, and where her personal reviews in *Anyone Can Whistle* were excellent, the production itself was commercially unsuccessful. Bowab even remembers having the telephone slammed in his ear when he would call potential investors with the idea of starring Lansbury in the show. "Of course these same people complained a year later saying, 'Why didn't you tell us the show was going to be so great?'"

From the very beginning, the producers and new director were at odds with each other about who to hire for the lead. Gene Saks wanted to cast his wife Beatrice Arthur, Joe and Sylvia Harris were adamant that Dolores Gray would be the ideal Mame. Four months after Lansbury's first audition, she finally decided to force the producers' hands. She flew to New York and auditioned for the show's new director, Gene Saks.

Lansbury recalled in the Hallowell *Life* article, "So in the morning I said, 'Right, this is it.' I told the prodcers, 'I am going back to California and unless you tell me – let's face it, I have prostrated myself – now, yes or no, that's the end of it.'"

After the lengthy casting search was concluded, and Lansbury's mandate, it had finally come down to a vote. Onna White, Jerry Herman, John Bowab and Lawrence and Lee nominated Angela Lansbury. Majority ruled. Lansbury remembers, "That afternoon Jimmy Carr came to my hotel and said, 'We are offering you *Mame*. It's official.'"

Jerry Herman promised to work with Lansbury on the music, Onna White said that she would coach Lansbury on the dances, and Bowab instinctively knew that she would bring a lovely, humorous, luminous honesty to the part.

On December 15, 1965, it was announced in the *New York Times* that Angela Lansbury had been chosen to star in the Broadway production of *Mame*.

*

"The lady-likeness of Angela was one of the important factors in her getting the role," says Onna White. "Mame is so lovable. She's not trashy. No matter what Mame does, it is always lady-like. Even her put-down barbs were done with subtle refinement."

149

As Mame Dennis, beautiful Angela Lansbury delighted audiences and critics alike with her show-stopping, Tony Award winning performance in the Broadway musical *Mame.* (Courtesy of Willard Waterman)

Casting the other company members was done with equal veracity. The *New York Journal American* reported that Kitty Carlisle would make her Broadway comeback as Vera Charles. However, brilliant comedienne Beatrice Arthur, who had created a sensation in 1964 in the role of Yente the Matchmaker in "Fiddler on the Roof," won the role. This was surely one of the foremost matches of actress and character ever conceived on Broadway!

Many young men would have been acceptable for the role of the Adult Patrick, except that in the novel Patrick's hero is Fred Astaire, and Jerry Herman had written a dance number named after the legendary dancer. Many otherwise suitable actors became unacceptable because they couldn't dance. Singer John Davidson had been chosen to play Patrick during the time that Mary Martin was expected to play Mame and before the Astaire song was written. He was a hot young singer at the time, but when they got around to actually doing the show, Davidson was engaged in other projects, including the CBS television variety series *The Entertainers.*

The producers ultimately cast Jerry Lanning, literally at the last minute. Another actor was only moments away from being offered the part when William Morris agent Phyllis Rab called the producer's office. "What's happening with the role of Patrick?" she queried. John Bowab explained that there was an actor over at the theatre, even as they were speaking, ready to sign a contract for the part.

"Hold on," Rab asserted. "I'm sending someone over in a cab right now. I want you to see him."

Within fifteen minutes, the office receptionist floated into Bowab's office and said, "I think I've just died. You've got to see the man that Phyllis has sent over..."

Jerry Lanning walked into the office and though Bowab remembers that he wasn't anything like what they originally had in mind for the Patrick Dennis character, Lanning was indeed striking in the good looks department.

"He had an open and honest soul," remembers the associate producer. "Though he looked like a rugged football player he had one of the great show voices."

Bowab picked up the telephone and called the Winter Garden Theatre. "Don't bring that boy for the Patrick Dennis character out on stage," he told the stage manager.

"But the actor knows he's got the part," the manager implored. "He's just waiting to be told 'thank you, we'll send a contract to your agent.'"

That actor later told Bowab that as soon as he saw Lanning walk through the stage door, he knew it was over for him.

The strong-voiced Jerry Lanning came from a solid theatrical background. His father, Don Lanning, had appeared on Broadway in such shows as *Good News* and *Artists & Models.* His mother was renowned nightclub singer Roberta Sherwood. Lanning had already made a strong public impression as a rising vocalist on the February 28, 1962 episode of *The Dick Van Dyke Show,* singing the novelty dance song, "The Twizzle" and a soaring rendition of "This Nearly Was Mine."

*

Sab Shimono, who portrayed Ito, wryly reported that when he first came to New York he pledged to himself, "The last thing I'll do is play a Japanese houseboy." A student at the University of California in the pre-med program, Shimono developed into an actor and his first Broadway part was in *Mame* – as Ito the houseboy! But Shimono soon learned that Ito was written as "a member of Mame's family," never servile or bowing.

Randy Kirby (son of *Candid Camera*'s Durwood Kirby) would

ultimately play the part of Junior Babcock for only three nights on Broadway as he was to leave to co-star in the NBC television series *The Girl from U.N.C.L.E.*

The role of Agnes Gooch had been consolidated to include both the myopic secretary who learns to "live" under Mame's tutelage, and the nursemaid Norah Muldoon. Jane Connell, who, in addition to her stage credits, was most popularly known for her appearances Saturday mornings on the *Captain Kangaroo* kiddie television show.

Connell started her career in a nightclub act with her husband Gordon in San Francisco. The team worked their way to New York, and after several Broadway revues, she created the role of Mrs. Peachum in *The Threepenny Opera*. Connell then appeared on Broadway in *New Faces of 1956*. She also starred in the London production of *Once Upon a Mattress*. For one season she was Sid Caesar's feminine foil on television in the comedian's series, *As Caesar Sees It*. She was also standby for Hermione Baddeley in *Cool Off*, a show which cooled off quickly during out-of-town try-outs at the Forrest Theatre. After ten years of being cast in several unsuccessful Broadway shows in a row, it looked as though *Mame* was going to break her long spell of disappointments in such production as *Drat the Cat*, and *Royal Flush*.

"I had played Gooch in a Sacramento summer tent production of the original play," Connell says, "so I dressed the way I thought Agnes would dress when I went in for my audition. I sang 'I Feel Pretty,' and dear Onna White, that one sole female voice out in the dark, said, 'Well, what more do you want!' I've always been grateful to her for that."

In the role of young Patrick Dennis, the producers found that rarity of the theatre, a child performer without any affectation. Young Frankie Michaels was already a veteran actor, having appeared in two off-Broadway productions, *A For Adult* and

Happily Ever After. He was also a regular on the daytime drama *As the World Turns.* Michaels' easy charm and abundant good nature astonished the producers as he gave the impression of being just a very nice kid who happens to sing and dance. By the time the show opened, he was being hailed as the theatre's first real juvenile counterpart to Shirley Temple, Mickey Rooney and Judy Garland.

It has been said that child actors in important roles are the chanciest of theatre chances. But Frankie Michaels was a surprisingly good performer. Without being saccharin, he was completely convincing in the role and earned accolades from the press that rivaled both Angela Lansbury's and Beatrice Arthur's notices. "I'm sure that Miss Lansbury would be the first to assert how difficult her job would be with a lesser nephew," one critic wrote, while another said, "Frankie Michaels proves conclusively that child actors need not be revolting."

Willard Waterman, as Patrick Dennis' puffy, pompous guardian, hailed from Madison, Wisconsin. In 1946, his popular radio show, *Those Websters,* moved from Chicago to Los Angeles, where he began his TV and movie career. In *Mame* he had a lively song called "Sterling Silver Boy" for his role as Dwight Babcock. But, in an effort to cut the show down to a reasonable length, that number was one of the casualties of paring the contents of the production. Well known for his radio and TV characterization of *The Great Gildersleeve* and in the film *Auntie Mame* (as Claude Upson), he appeared in 30 movies including *It's a Mad, Mad, Mad, Mad World, The Apartment, Three Coins in the Fountain* and *Fourteen Hours.*

CHAPTER SEVEN

From Rehearsal to Opening Night

"I CAN'T BELIEVE IT," Lansbury said in an interview at the time of her being cast as Mame Dennis. "I wanted something like this to happen. It's quite mysterious and quite eerie in the way it did happen. I'm the most fulfilled person."

The *Mame* company was a serene and yet hardworking group primarily because of Angela Lansbury's theatrical integrity and persona. The rehearsal period was a happy and relatively easy one for the entire company.

"I don't want to sound like a blathering fool, but it was absolutely the best experience I ever had in the theatre," notes Jerry Herman of the rehearsals and out-of-town tryouts of *Mame* in Philadelphia and Boston. "It's [out-of-town] supposed to be the most grueling, terrifying experience – and I have a lot of those stories from other shows – but in Philadelphia we literally went to the movies. We cut about 15 minutes and then Lawrence and Lee and I took Angela and Bea to the movies."

With a show as physically demanding as *Mame*, Lansbury realized she was in for a great deal of work. She knew that performing in eight shows a week would be a grind, and she was determined to maintain her health.

"I prepared for the role like a boxer for a heavyweight fight," Lansbury said at the time. "Exercise, special food, ballet...otherwise I would lack luster, I assure you," she said. "I survived the London Blitz, quite possibly I can survive all this. I just can't tell yet how much energy I'm going to need. The whole thing is

Angela Lansbury starring in the title role of *Mame*. (Courtesy of Willard Waterman)

being plotted very carefully so I don't have to keep running around out of breath."

In addition to taking part in 11 songs, a rare number even for an Ethel Merman or Mary Martin, Miss Lansbury's assignment included much dancing and 20 costume changes.

Singer/dancer/actor Ron Young, who portrayed the character Ralph Devine, remembers that they rehearsed at the old Variety Arts building in Manhattan. "Angela had such energy," Young says. "She's not really a trained dancer, but she has such a feel for dancing. In her opening number, she did a jitterbug and I did back flips with her. She did one thing I'll ways remember. She would fall back into my arms and kick her foot above her head. I always had to make sure my head was on the other side because she was so extended that she would overshoot her shoulder. I would get her foot in my face if my head was in the wrong place."

Speaking with the director Gene Saks and his wife Beatrice Arthur, Whitney Bolton of the *Philadelphia Inquirer* got the scoop on how rehearsals were coming along. Bolton's article refealed that, according to Saks and Arthur, their working together had turned out quite well but they revealed one amusing incident that occurred. "We had to give up a gimmick we had planned for the first day of rehearsal," Saks acknowledged. "What we planned was that at the first reading by the cast, with all of us sitting around, I would not interrupt or correct anyone else but would interrupt and curtly correct Beatrice after every line she uttered. I was to become progressively rude and she was to become progressively more resistant, resentful and finally outraged. But we were chicken when the time came. We feared the impact on the rest of the cast. It seemed to us that it might backfire."

As in the original production of *Auntie Mame* starring Rosalind Russell, elaborate clothes were an important part of the star's wardrobe in *Mame*. Robert Mackintosh was given the task of creating nearly 275 costumes for the new musical.

Following on the heels of the reputation that Russell had for wearing striking gowns, it was determined that Miss Lansbury's wardrobe had to be equally exciting. "I thought it would be fun to make the clothes look like Hollywood glamour rather than exact representations of the period," Mackintosh explained. "Besides, nobody wanted the eight inches from the ground length of the 1920s and '30s. Mame Dennis is an uninhibited extrovert when it comes to clothes. When Rosalind Russell did the play on Broadway, she had 17 costumes designed by Travis Banton. She had 10 to 30 seconds to change into them. Miss Lansbury had to make her changes in 10 to 15 seconds."

Mackintosh revealed that because of the requirements for changing costumes, he had to provide some tricky snaps, zippers and pop-open clothes. "To illustrate Mame's nature, she wears sable trimmed suits, gold-palliated pajamas, a silver lamé coat lined with monkey fur and a white dress swathed in blue fox fur."

*

On March 27, 1966, the cast of *Mame* took to the pre-Broadway road. They arrived in Philadelphia to prepare for a three-week run at the Shubert Theatre before going on to Boston. The cast promptly and collectively came down with the flu.

"I remember thinking I was quite possibly going to die," remembers Margaret Hall who portrayed southern belle Sally Cato. "Angela was ill and they had microphones that looked like cobras, they stood up so high, to pick up her weak voice. Her understudy, Charlotte Fairchild, was ready to go on but I'm sure Angela felt an obligation to go on even if she had to crawl."

There was no way to speculate whether or not this show was going to be a hit. "During the process of rehearsal, everything was an unknown factor," Jane Connell remembers. "Many things worried me about the show. For instance, there weren't any dominant men, the roles were really all strong women. That rather bothered me."

But there were several very dominant men involved with the show. However, they were all behind the scenes: the producers, director, playwrights and composer. Their strength was revealed in both noble leadership and the wielding of omnipotent power over the production. Collectively, they had the muscle to make or break *Mame*, and it was later revealed that they were even considering replacing Angela Lansbury. Until opening night in Philadelphia, some still weren't convinced that she could carry the show.

Ron Young remembers the very first orchestra rehearsal at the Shubert in Philadelphia: "We had been working with just a piano in the basement of a hotel two blocks from the theatre. When we finally got on stage for the first time and it came time for Angela to sing her big ballad, 'If He Walked Into My Life,' Angela was sitting there on stage next to Jerry Herman, and Don Pippin was conducting. The way Phil Lang had orchestrated the number it was to start with a reed instrument on a solo line, in a very plaintive melody just before Angela starts to sing. Well, the reed instrument played – and Angela burst into tears and threw her arms around Jerry. She was so happy and appreciative."

Angela Lansbury had been in the entertainment business for many years and was considered a star, but not a star of great magnitude. After playing "second ladies" all her professional life, she was well aware that *Mame* had the potential to catapult her to the front ranks.

"I love it," Lansbury said to John Hallowell in *Life* magazine. "Hell, I want all the glamor there is. I've been starving for it for years! People forget I made a movie musical in 1945 called *The Harvey Girls*. It was marked by the fact that I was mean to Judy Garland in it."

Choreographer Onna White remembers that while rehearsing the title song she had a brainstorm. She called director Gene Saks aside and said, "During this number, while the cast is singing to Mame, I would like to put Angie facing the cast, her back to the audience."

Saks was incredulous. "The star with her back to the audience?! I'm not going to tell a leading lady to put her back to the audience," he flinched. "You'll have to tell her."

"Angie," White called out, "don't think I'm crazy. You're such a good actress and I have an idea that I know you can pull off. I would like you to stand here, stage right, with your *back* to the audience, and let the cast sing to you." Always the consummate, trusting professional, Lansbury simply said, "Fine. Wherever you want me to stand is fine."

An amusing incident resulted from this tactic. White recalls that one night after a performance in Boston, she received a call to come to the front of the house. When she arrived, Barbara Stanwyck was waiting for her. "I came all the way here to meet the person who told a leading lady to put her *back* to the audience," Stanwyck cracked.

That musical number, *Mame*, literally stopped the show on opening night in Philadelphia. White remembers that on one occasion she went backstage after the song to find tears running down Lansbury's face. The audiences' response had been so great that Lansbury could actually feel their love for her. She was overcome with happiness.

Yet, earlier that night, Onna White and Gene Saks received a call from Lansbury's husband, Peter Shaw. "Would you come right over?" he implored. "Angela is so scared, so frightened. You've got to talk to her." White remembers that she went to Lansbury's hotel, and the star was, indeed apprehensive about facing the audience. "We talked to her, encouraged her and finally she pulled herself together. Of course she was wonderful opening night!"

The show opened and was an enormous success. However, the production ran 35 minutes too long that first night and cuts had to be made. Equal amounts of dialogue and song were very carefully excised by the authors themselves to make up the time they needed. Among the musical portions painstakingly excised was a number entitled "Camouflage" which was a duet between Mame and Vera Charles in Mame's bedroom as she prepares to meet the banker Babcock. Another, "Sterling Silver

Boy," sung by Babcock, and a ballad entitled "Love Is Only Love" (which turned up later in the motion picture version of *Hello, Dolly!*) also were removed.

Each of the numbers was wonderful in its own right, but in *Mame* they became stage "waits" and held up the show. They didn't allow the proceedings to flow smoothly, so in Philadelphia they were judiciously removed.

The musical *Mame* was produced for roughly $500,000, a hefty chunk of capital at that time. But it paid back its entire investment in only 24 weeks, a remarkably short duration. Despite the show's success, however, it was never a big money-maker because it was an extremely heavy show in terms of maintenance.

John Bowab says, "It wasn't like doing a *Fiddler on the Roof* where if a costume got a rip in it you just sewed it back up. The *Mame* production had two women who did nothing but sew sequins back onto Lansbury's dresses."

In addition to the operating cost of the show, the royalty structure was extremely exorbitant, possibly as high as any musical ever because they were paying off not only Patrick Dennis, but also the original producers (even though they were now co-producing the new show). They were also paying off Lawrence and Lee as the original writers, and, of course, they had the high-priced composer Jerry Herman. As part of the termination deal for Josh Logan, he also received a percentage of the gross. In addition, Warner Bros. got a slice of the box office pie.

After three and a half weeks of successful performances in Philadelphia, the cast and crew packed their trunks and headed to the Shubert Theatre in Boston. Both *Mame* and Fryer, Carr and Harris' other hit, *Sweet Charity*, had been such a major attraction that the producers took a full page ad in the Philadelphia papers expressing their appreciation to the theatergoers of that town:

"Thank you, Philadelphia, for your warm and overwhelming reception. We are sorry to have disappointed so many of our friends seeking tickets, but previous commitments in both instances prevented a longer stay." At $77,600, *Mame* had set a box-office record at the Shubert in Philadelphia.

A critic's job is to criticize, but if the writers had listened to the pundits, and not maintained their theatrical integrity, some of the best material might have been irrevocably tampered with. For instance, when *Mame* opened at the Shubert Theatre in Boston on April 28, the reviewer at the *Christian Science Monitor* noted that the second act should be changed. "Like her earlier incarnations in the novel, as a play and on screen, *Auntie Mame* is tinged by a touch of vulgarity," the Boston critic noted. "Act II is upstaged by Act I. A partial solution might be to end Act I with 'The Moon Song,' and cut Miss Lansbury's 'If He Walked Into My Life' it would never be missed."

So much for the learned opinions of the so-called experts. "If He Walked Into My Life" became one of the most popular songs from the show and a bona-fide standard. Jerry Herman recalls that he wrote the song to be sung by an aunt to her nephew. However, "Eydie Gormé made it into a torch song without changing one syllable of what I wrote, and won a Grammy Award and people all over the country thought it was a song written about a relationship between a guy and a girl."

On April 17, 1966 Eydie Gormé recorded "If He Walked Into My Life" for her Columbia album *Don't Go to Strangers.* It became a hit even before the show reached Broadway, and Bobby Darin, Louis Armstrong (with revised lyrics by Jerry Herman), Al Hirt and Pearl Bailey were already on the charts with the title song, "Mame."

Ensconced in his suite at the Statler Hotel in Boston, composer Jerry Herman explained to reporter Samuel Hirsh the company's methodology for preparing *Mame* for Broadway. "The production staff watches each performance and meets afterwards to compare notes and decide on changes," the composer related. "It's a fascinating process, like a wonderful jigsaw puzzle we're trying to put together. We're conscious of the pieces that are missing, or don't exactly fit, and we never stop trying to fill in the big picture. Now we're hoping the Boston audiences will help us by showing us what works and what we still need to change. We're looking for reactions that are universal because we believe that what works in Boston and Philadelphia and New York, should also work in Lincoln, Nebraska."

Elliot Norton, then considered the dean of the Boston critics, made an interesting observation in his newspaper column: "A few years ago, no producer would have been able to raise money for *Mame* because it is based on *Auntie Mame*, which has already been done, very successfully, as a motion picture. Until Rodgers and Hammerstein proved it was silly, the angels of Broadway wouldn't support a play or a musical which already had screen exposure. The screen rights of a successful play can bring a big price and a huge profit. So the custom has been to play first on the stage, then offer it to Hollywood. Then Rodgers and Hammerstein used the movie *Anna and the King of Siam* as the basis of their stage musical *The King and I*. Then they sold it for an enormous amount of money to picture producers who made it into a movie all over again. So another taboo, based as most theatrical taboos are, on insufficient evidence, was successfully discredited. With this fourth re-telling of the Patrick Dennis story, *Mame* is still in its infancy as a usable story."

The next morning (April 29, 1966), Kevin Kelly of the *Boston Globe* announced "*Mame* is unquestionably the best musical of the season. Angela Lansbury plays the title role as though she were the Crowned Queen of Camp, but with a superb sense of restraint. Miss Lansbury's talent has long been conceded, but her sudden appearance as a fabulous musical comedy performer is a revelation."

Kelly went on to praise the Lawrence and Lee book as "genuinely funny, the brightest book for a musical in many a dull musical moon." He added, "Under the well-paced direction of Gene Saks, the cast is perfect. Beatrice Arthur is venomously witty

Angela Lansbury (right) triumphed as Mame Dennis and received the 1966 Tony Award as Best Actress in a Musical. Frankie Michaels (left) also received a Tony Award. Jane Connell and Sab Shimono also starred. (Courtesy of Jerome Lawrence)

as Vera Charles; Jane Connell is achingly funny as Agnes Gooch."

It was admitted that a musical Mame is a more difficult role than her straight play cousin. In addition to acting, the lady in the lead role must also sing and dance. Critic Elliot Norton begrudgingly gave Lansbury credit as a professional with stage presence, and a tart, sharp way with comedy. "Miss Lansbury can't sing," he said, trying to balance his faint praise, "but then neither can anybody else in *Mame*. But she gets through most of the songs without ruining the melodies." The venerable critic stood alone in his remarks about the vocal contributions of the cast.

*

It was Tuesday, May 24, 1966. The advance ticket sales for *Mame* were already over $1 million and as the *New York Post* said, "Angela Lansbury has 'em lined up outside the Winter Garden box office like Piccadily Circus for Queen Victoria's coronation."

As curtains simultaneously went up behind prosceniums all along the pearly "Great White Way" for such popular attractions as Herschel Bernardi in *Fiddler on the Roof* at the Imperial Theatre, Henry Fonda in *Generation* at the Morosco, Lerner & Lane's musical *On a Clear Day You Can See Forever* with Barbara Harris and John Cullum at the Mark Hellinger, *Sweet Charity* at the Palace, and Neil Simon's *The Odd Couple* at the Plymouth Theatre, the cast of *Mame* was nervously preparing to confront their opening night Broadway audience.

Located on the site of the old American Horse Exchange, the Winter Garden had become a theatrical institution over the years. It was in this historic theatre at a Sunday-night concert that Al Jolson first sang Gershwin's "Swanee," Marilyn Miller, prior to her Ziegfeld Follies fame appeared dazzlingly in a "Passing Show" revue, and Kitty Gordon, known for her beautiful back and shoulders, was a radiant Winter Garden star.

In Jerry Herman's revealing autobiography *Show Tune*, he recalled an amusing opening night anecdote. As Don Pippin, Herman's musical director, was making his way to the orchestra pit he noticed his father seated in the third row. "He gave his father a little nod of recognition," Herman wrote. "The elder Mr. Pippin was so thrilled that he turned to the gray-haired gentleman sitting next to him, who was an absolute stranger, and said, 'That's my son conducting.' The stranger smiled back and said, 'He's conducting my son's music.'"

On cue, Donald Pippin raised his baton in the orchestra pit of the recently refurbished Winter Garden and started the rousing overture to Jerry Herman's score for *Mame*, and the house filled with applause.

As the curtain rose, two forlorn people, (Frankie Michaels and Jane Connell), representing Mame's nephew Patrick and his frumpy, owlish governess Agnes Gooch, sang "Saint Bridgette," a sly musical prayer for safe deliverance to Beekman Place and the loving arms of a dear, sweet Auntie Mame, as they arrive in New York. As everyone in the audience knew, Patrick and Agnes had come to the wrong address if they expected a gray-haired, cherry-pie-baking brand of aunt. When they eventually come face to face with the truth, they've entered a den of iniquity and a rollicking cocktail party.

As the gala continued, the audience waited for Angela Lansbury to appear, which she soon did – dressed in gold-palliated pajamas—making her long-awaited entrance at the top of a graceful, spiral staircase designed by William and Jean Eckart. As an uninhibited party swirled below her in the Beekman Place apartment, Mame blew a trumpet and happily observed, "All my dearest friends are here, even the ones I haven't met yet!" Thus, Angela Lansbury's position as the toast of Broadway began.

By the end of the evening when Lansbury took her final curtain call in a long white coat wrapped in white fox, comparisons
with Rosalind Russell were pointless. As Richard Coe of the
Washington Post observed, "Standing ovations are rare at New
York first nights, but that was exactly the reward for radiant
Angela Lansbury at the premiere of *Mame*. Miss Lansbury was
already a star but the reception as the musicalized Auntie Mame
sealed the technicality."

When Rosalind Russell first played Auntie Mame, it was
thought by all that the character would be hers forever. But in the
canny adaptation of their original play, Lawrence and Lee, along
with composer Jerry Herman, created a gentler Mame, a quieter
lady whose contempt for hypocrisy is actually stronger. It was
almost unanimously agreed that although Lansbury was not the
original Auntie Mame, she now owned the part completely.

Angela Lansbury's husband Peter Shaw, and their two children sat in the theatre opening night and proud tears rolled
down their cheeks as the first night audience gave their favorite
lady a clamorous standing ovation. Lansbury had stopped the
show several times – stopped it cold in the way Ethel Merman
and Mary Martin did in their finest musical moments.

Mame was a great opportunity for Angela Lansbury who had
the skill to build a complicated and interesting, tough but liber-
al lady. "How can I tell you what a staggering victory *Mame* is
for me?" Lansbury told author/critic Rex Reed in an interview
that appeared in the much admired writer's *Do You Sleep in the
Nude*? "I always suspected I could reach everybody, but I never
did until now. I always knew I would hit on something that
would unlock all the doors and hit all those people between the
eyes. Don't get me wrong. My career has been very satisfying
and a lot of wonderful people have dug what I've tried to do.
When I did *Anyone Can Whistle* – a magnificent failure – the

crowed yelled bravo, too. But that was the insy-poo New York crowd. They're marvelous, but they fizzle out after six weeks. I'm out to get the taxi drivers, shop ladies, and people on the street. Even teenagers are paying $9.50 a seat to see *Mame*. They love this dame. I hope the way I play her she's more than just a song and dance. She's all the women I've played. I'm like a sponge. Everything I see is ducated away in my pores. I've known a lot of Mames in my day and underneath they all cry 'Need me.' It's taken me forty-one years, but I've finally found a role that is the sum total of everything I know and everybody's digging me for the first time."

In the crazy atmosphere of the Rainbow Room for a post-show celebration, the attendees "brava-ed" the reading of the reviews. No one was surprised to learn that Angela Lansbury was an accomplished actress, but not everyone knew she could also sing and dance. She combined all of these elements into a musical performance in a marathon role that had critics raving. As one critic pointed out, "Without Angela Lansbury the show would be a bright, satisfying evening of musical theatre; with her, it's tossed virtually into ensemble orbit."

Jack O'Brien, on his *The Voice of Broadway* broadcast on May 25, described the opening night performance thus: "*Mame* is better than merely good, and where it needs a little life, Angela Lansbury switches on the jet-assisted-takeoff of her talents and personality and flings it higher than it rightfully might expect.

"With Beatrice Arthur as Miss Lansbury's sidekick, the second act starts whirling like John Glenn in a song called 'Bosom Buddies,' in which they stress that only such life-long pals possibly could analyze each others' faults, age, drinking, sex and other indoor sports and still stay bosom buddies."

Stan Page, who performed in the cast as the elevator boy, and later began serving as stage manager during the run of the show, remembers one evening when he timed the pause that Bea Arthur makes as Vera Charles after the reprise of the "Bosom Buddies" number:

Vera: I've patiently watched you for years
　　　With these asinine projects of yours:
　　　From orphans to health foods, you've searched for a
　　　niche.
Mame: I feel that my search will be over
　　　The moment I've finished my book.
　　　I'll write about us —
　　　And who is the bitchier bitch.
Vera: (after eleven second pause): I concede.

"Bea held the audience in her hand," Page recalls. "No sound …no movement…for eleven seconds – with just her look. Then the words 'I concede.'" "She held them there and it was magnificent. And at the end of the number, naturally they got tremendous applause."

Jack O'Brien continued his praise, "Miss Lansbury definitely is the season's most terrific toast of Broadway. In this, the final production of the theatrical season, not only is she better than any other musical star, but better than all the rest this season combined.

"The show got off to a nice if not spectacular start with a good, enjoyable, hardly earth-shattering first act, but the second act, in an era of so-so second acts, came on like gangbusters produced by Superman, Batman and the Green Hornet. Jane Connell was hilariously hopeless as Agnes Gooch; Beatrice Arthur as the wry, tough, witchy, high-style vixen of a great stage star dipped in liquor, might have stolen the show from anyone except Angela Lansbury. Frankie Michaels as 10-year-old Patrick, Mame's nephew and happy new hobby, could not have been better, never once a stage brat; he sings louder than everyone and better than most."

On May 31, 1966, The League of New York Theatres in conjunction with the American Theatre Wing, announced the contenders for that season's annual Tony Awards. Four nominees in each of sixteen categories from 50 productions were selected by critics Judith Crist, Lee Jordan, Norman Nadel and Tom Prideaux; broadcasting executive Donald Flamm; and theatrical lighting company president Edward Kook, to be voted upon by 500 theatre people.

When the votes were tallied for the 1965-66 Tony Awards, presented June 16, 1966 at The Rainbow Room at Rockefeller Center, *Mame* and *Man of La Mancha* were the runaway successes, garnering awards for Angela Lansbury (Outstanding Musical Actress), Beatrice Arthur and Frankie Michael (Outstanding Musical Actress/Actor, Supporting or Featured.) *Mame*'s other nominations were Outstanding Musical, Outstanding Composer and Lyricist, Outstanding Director, Outstanding Choreographer and Outstanding Scenic Designer.

According to Lee Alan Morrow's *The Tony Award Book* (New York: Abbeville Press, 1987): "Owing to the recent death of Helen Mencken, the president of the American Theatre Wing, the awards ceremony featured no entertainment and was held, for the only time, during the afternoon.

"For the first time, the awards were not voted on by the membership of the American Theatre Wing, but the vote was given to members of the first and second-night press lists, and the governing boards of Actors Equity the Dramatists Guild, and the Society of Stage Directors and Choreographers."

It was stunning acclaim for Lansbury. After 20 years of doing second leads, being nominated three times for the Academy Award, but never winning, she took the seasonal Tony Award home with her that night.

*

After 775 performances on Broadway, it was announced that Angela Lansbury would be leaving the cast. Though a replacement at the time of the departure notice had yet to be found, the producers were considering numerous potential stars.

Margaret Hall, who portrayed Southern Belle Sally Cato, remembers Lansbury's tear-filled final performance: "All the ensemble players brought in yellow and white flowers, and for Angela's final bow, we all strewed the stage with them so that she walked across a floral carpet. It was truly kept a secret, she had no idea this was going to happen and her face just crumpled, she was so overwhelmed. Then she went to the middle of the stage, hushed the audience and said, "I expect that you know that this has been the biggest love-in in town."

Hall remembers that although Lansbury was quite protective of the bugle she used in the show, somehow several cast members were able to substitute it with another, and had the original engraved. They presented the sentimental treasure to Lansbury at the going away party held at the CBS Black Rock Building on 6th Avenue the night of her farewell performance.

*

Casting the replacement for Angela Lansbury proved to be one of the more interesting aspects of *Mame*. Celeste Holm had taken over the lead role during one of Lansbury's two week vacations and prior to heading the national tour, and had garnered ecstatic notices including one from *New York Times* critic Dan Sullivan who said, "In sum, Miss Holm makes an aunt that every little boy would love to have..."

A star's replacement in a hit Broadway show is pivotally

171

important but doesn't usually warrant the attention garnered by the creator of the role. Many stars wanted the plum role of Mame as much as Lansbury had wanted the role originally. Judy Garland was among them.

"For Garland to come into Lansbury's hit show was an ironic concept," says associate producer John Bowab, "considering that she had been the star of the MGM musical *The Harvey Girls* in which Angela had been merely a supporting player in 1945."

However, in 1967, Garland – who would be dead in two years at age 47 from an accidental overdose of sleeping pills – was battling failing health, dependence on prescription medication, and bankruptcy – the latter the result of duplicitous business advisors and managers who had – over the preceding decade – placed her in debt for more than half a million dollars. Judy had only recently lost her Brentwood, California home, selling it at the last moment to avoid foreclosure by the Internal Revenue Service.

But for all of her career ups and downs, in autumn 1967 Garland was again at a relatively high point in her later career. She had, in August, closed a triumphant third Broadway engagement at the Palace Theatre and, on either side of that booking had successfully completed scores of concerts without missing a performance. Still, her personal and professional legend was erratic.

When it was made known to the producers that Garland wanted to audition for the part, they arranged for her to attend a performance of the show before coming in to meet with them. What they perhaps did not know is that she had already seen the show several times in early 1967.

According to respected Garland biographer John Fricke, Judy first visited *Mame* from seats front-row center at the Winter Garden during a trip to New York City in January 1967. Afterward, she and escort/publicist (later-fiancé) Tom Green, and his sister and brother-in-law visited Angela backstage. Two weeks later Judy returned for a second visit and asked if she could watch from the wings, anxious to see the backstage workings of the production. The stage manager, worried that she might be crushed in the mad, on-and-off-stage rush of performers, crew, and scenery, had to decline. When in New York again for daughter Liza Minnelli's wedding in March, Garland saw the show a third time.

In June, she opened her first concert stand in nearly a year at the Westbury (Long Island, New York) Music Fair. On opening night, after "I Feel a Song Comin' On" and her "Almost Like Being in Love"/"This Can't Be Love" medley, Garland announced, "We have some new songs." Paramount among these was the orchestration she'd had prepared for "If He Walked Into My Life." But – unsure of and unfamiliar with the new arrangement – Judy forsook the number after two or three brief attempts. "I think Angela Lansbury should sing this herself" was Garland's blithe comment when one go at the song trailed off in confusion between the singer, conductor, and musicians.

Although her initial rendition of the first few lines was, in the words of one listener, "meltingly beautiful," Judy ultimately countered with, "Let's do 'San Francisco,'" feeling much more at home with one of her own familiar standards. Garland's orchestration of "If He Walked Into My Life" remained with her charts for another year, but she never again attempted to sing it in concert performance.

More than two decades later, when Jerry Herman was informed of Garland's Westbury effort, he commented, "I was told she didn't have enough rehearsal and was wise enough to know that. She was doing it very raw. She was such a perfectionist and such an artist, she must have sensed that."

Judy, however, already had more than a passing familiarity

with Herman's score for *Mame* which she patently adored. On March 12, 1967, a *Chicago American* newspaper writer related the story of a recent evening he'd spent in Hollywood at a private party where Garland had been prevailed upon to sing; including "the score of *Mame* virtually completed." He noted that Judy wanted to play the role and added, "It should rejoice her loving legion of fans to know she is a major contender for the film version, whenever it comes along."

In October 1967, while on her post-Palace concert tour, Judy was again quoted on the subject of the property during an interview with a reporter in Hartford, Connecticut: "She'd 'love' to play the leading role in the projected screen version of the Broadway hit, *Mame*. To her knowledge, no one's been signed yet. 'The field's still wide open,' Judy said. 'The role's the kind that contains a tremendous excitement to me as a performer.'"

Like so many other *name* actresses interested in replacing Lansbury, Judy felt that by doing the part she might get a chance to do the film version of *Mame*. Fricke says that throughout her career, Garland had expressed interest in doing a Broadway musical or play, rather than the "personal appearance" revues in which she appeared, like at The Palace and Metropolitan Opera House. *Mame* would have been ideal.

A meeting between the producers and Garland eventually took place in October 1967, and Jerry Herman was present to play the score for her. "She sang everything in the show, and it just put us away," recalls John Bowab. "It was beyond comprehension what she did with the score. When she sang 'If He Walked Into My Life,' 'We Need a Little Christmas,' 'My Best Beau' and 'It's Today,' it was simply devastating. She must have had the pitch pipes out all night because there wasn't a crack in her voice, except when she wanted it to crack."

Despite Garland's brilliance, there was a major fear among

the producers that she couldn't sustain eight performances a week over an extended period of time. *Mame* was an enormous hit and there was a strong apprehension that she might kill the show altogether. If the production had been in its third or fourth year, it is likely she would have been given a chance, but the producers felt they couldn't risk potential problems.

Judy was told in late January 1968 that she'd lost the role. Distraught and self-condemning, she was taken that evening by her then son-in-law Peter Allen to daughter Liza's supper club act at a New York hotel. Liza bolstered her mother's spirits by inviting her to take stage for their "family duet" of "When the Saints Go Marchin' In"/"Brotherhood of Man," and Judy soloed with the Gershwins/Kahn song from which she'd selected her daughter's name. The audience was rapturous, and Judy's faith in herself was briefly restored.

"It broke my heart that Garland wasn't hired," Bowab says. "To me, it would have been worth it if she opened and closed after one night and she never did the show again. Jerry Herman felt that way, as did Lawrence and Lee."

Judy Garland's reaction to her rejection bordered on sheer desperation, according to Bowab. "I guess the only phone number she had was mine. I don't think the woman slept for three or four days because she would call me at two in the afternoon, seven at night, one in the morning and again at six a.m. She kept blaming [former husband] Sid Luft, saying that he probably told us that she wouldn't be able to make it. I kept insisting that we never talked to Sid Luft. Then she accused her [former] agents, David Begelman and Freddie Fields, of sabotaging her. She was looking for any excuse other than her own reputation. I tried to explain that we just saw another image for the part – which wasn't true – but I couldn't tell the lady that nobody felt she could do the job.

"It was strange for me, this kid from Pawtucket, Rhode Island, telling the great Judy Garland that 'no, you can't have the job,' for a role that I think she was perfectly suited. I think she would have been a sensation as Mame."

Offering a corroborated rumor heard many years ago, John Fricke reveals he was told by an investigative journalist that it was Judy's doctor and lawyer who intervened with producers Fryer, Carr, and Harris. The producers were so seriously considering Garland as Lansbury's replacement that the doctor and lawyer stepped in, quietly and off-the record, to ask them *not* to hire her. Their professional opinion was that Judy's health would never permit her to sustain the production, and that should she commit to the show and then have to be replaced (or begin the run and then start missing performances), her reputation would be further damaged.

Jerry Herman was equally melancholy about the turn of events. He was and remains Garland's self-avowed number one fan. In 1975, he reminisced, "What a shame she never knew how much I owe to her. Judy was the personification of the show business that I love and understand – and I have, for years, kept her voice unconsciously in my brain as I compose…very often influencing my choice of a word or a note. So you see, much of *my* sound and much of *my* style I owe to Judy Garland."

Years later, Herman said, "She inspired me in ways nobody knows. I heard her singing 'It's Today' when I was writing it, because that's a very 'Garland song.' It was perfect for her. That kind of theatrical, emotional show business has affected my life and my work. She's 'there.'"

Even while considering Judy Garland, the producers auditioned other actresses as Lansbury's replacement. Jane Wyman came in and sang "You Made Me Love You" (ironically, a Garland trademark song), but the producers didn't think she had enough stage experience. Shirl Conway was a big star from the television show *The Nurses* and she had starred on Broadway in *Plain and Fancy*. She gave a great audition but again, the producers didn't think she was strong enough. The list of talents who wanted the role went on and on. Finally, Janis Paige, who had starred in numerous Broadway hits including *The Pajama Game, Here's Love* and *It Remains To Be Seen*, came in and read and sang for the part. She appeared to be everything the producers had been looking for, and was signed for the coveted role.

*

On Wednesday October 18, 1968, *Mame* played its 1,000th performance at the Winter Garden Theatre, becoming only the 18th musical in theatrical history to attain this lofty achievement.

Esteemed theatre critic Clive Barnes appraised the show and the new Mame Janis Paige's performance in his April 20th review saying, "Janis Paige has now become Mame in place of Angela Lansbury, and she is making an excellent job of it. She looks glowingly well, and sings, dances and acts with a sweet enthusiasm, but not perhaps the bittersweet enthusiasm Miss Lansbury presented. She's less of a character but, as some compensation, perhaps more of a performer."

Barnes acknowledged that in the two years since he had seen *Mame* with Lansbury his feeling for the show had been elevated by the lack of quality in other productions playing in town. "*Mame* arrived on Broadway nearly two years ago, and I remember thinking at the time you have to sit through the entire first act to get to the hit song, and then when it comes it sounds like *Hello Dolly!* Well, I've personally suffered a lot of other musicals since those happy days of innocence, and believe me, *Mame* seems all the better by contrast. It remains

177

one of the best musicals of the past few seasons."

His review also noted that few if any of the original cast remained with the show, "among them, Helen Gallagher, who has come in as Gooch, would be an asset to almost any show, and she is brilliantly amusing here."

Barnes couldn't quite summon any words of commendation for Audrey Christie who starred as Vera Charles.

After eight months, singer/actress Jane Morgan took over the role from Janis Paige. Again Clive Barnes reviewed the production: "It is slowly dawning upon me that certain musicals are going to be with us – like the poor – forever," he began. "I can see myself, three quarters blind, totally toothless, largely deaf, staggering up to a musical like *Mame* in about 25 years' time to review Judy Garland's grand-daughter in the title role.

"...But I should complain? If you're going to have to see a musical four times (and I am just starting in the job) *Mame* does stand up better than most. It is still, almost three years after the start, one of the more entertaining musicals in town. We have now had three Mames – to say nothing of the stand-by Sheila Smith, who has filled in on numerous occasions – and the role is seemingly foolproof, although this remark is not meant to sound as ungracious to the ladies in question as it doubtless does.

"The newest Mame," he continued, "is Jane Morgan, who brings to the proceedings a strong voice and a well-projected stage personality. She appears to be a tougher lady than some of her predecessors, belting out the songs with all the well-honed expertise of someone very used to singing for her supper. This is a good-natured show-biz style portrayal that fits well with the musical."

Barnes's comments of Anne Francine, as Mame's bosom buddy Vera Charles, was almost a rejoice that Audrey Christie was gone from the show. "The new Vera Charles ... plays the first lady-lush of the American stage with a sodden dignity and a very properly gin-soaked croak."

Finally, after four years of standing-room-only performances, *Mame* was beginning to look rather ragged and it appeared the production would soon be closing. "I felt a few tautening rehearsals by the director Gene Saks would not have come amiss," Clive Barnes had reported the year before.

Then, associate producer John Bowab had a brainstorm. He had directed Ann Miller in Zev Buffman's production of *Mame* at the Royal Ponciana Playhouse in Florida. The reviews had been sensational and he thought, "What if she were to come to Broadway?"

The *Miami Herald* had said, "The lithe and radiant Ann Miller is the perfect song-and-dance version of the famous folk heroine." The *Hollywood Florida Tattler* raved, "Ann Miller is Mame, the beautiful; Mame, the enchantress; Mame, the incorrigible spoiler of her nephew; a captivating Mame."

Bowab, supported by such unusually strong notices, including the *Miami Beach Reporter's* ovation, "We were flabbergasted by the caliber of Miss Miller's performance. She showed talents we never knew she had. Her dancing, of course, has never been questioned, but her style and quality as a performer has never had a chance to prove itself before. She is as good a Mame as they make, and we fell in love with her from the first moment she appeared," decided to risk a seemingly wild idea.

As Bowab recalls, "I called Jerry Herman and the producers and said, 'I know this is a gamble, but the reaction to Ann is unbelievable. I know she's nobody's idea of what Mame is, she's a jazzier Texan type, but she's funny and warm and sings the bejesus out of the score.'"

The producers and Jerry Herman flew down to Florida to see Miller in the role and they all agreed she was terrific. As the New York production was on the verge of closing anyway, they had little to lose by bringing Miller to Broadway.

"I walked out onto that stage without any rehearsal," remembers Ann Miller of her New York debut. "I'd never seen the props, or done a proper run-through with the orchestra. But I knocked 'em dead! It was a big moment for me."

"The reviews were as strong as the ones Angela got," John Bowab remembers. "I think the singing is what stunned everybody. Ann was an actress who had not done a movie in 13 or 14 years and nobody knew she could sing."

Miller remembers that authors Lawrence and Lee were absolute task masters when it came to her speaking their lines. "I had the habit of adding my own little words, like 'oh,' 'well' and 'but.' They insisted that I say the line as written; nothing in front of it. They watched me like a snake would watch a bird to make sure I didn't put anything in there that didn't belong. They were right. My adding things was throwing off the timing, then I started getting bigger laughs."

Most famous as one of the greatest tap dancers of all time, Miller could not step out onto a stage in a musical without displaying her legendary dance skills. Choreographer Onna White's assistant Diana Baffa had given Miller a short tap routine to do in the Florida production, which came after the "That's How Young I Feel" song. For Broadway, White expanded the tap number for Miller and the crowds walked away fulfilled.

One amusing anecdote recited by cast members recalls a potentially hazardous incident that turned out funny. It seems that during one of the performances, Ann was struck by the big crescent moon set. The stage manager insisted that she complete a worker's compensation form, in case there were any future complications from what appeared to be a minor accident. He brought out his clipboard and went down the list of questions on the insurance form: "Name," he asked in a professional manner.

"Ann Miller," the entertainer replied.

"Occupation?"

"Star," Miller said. Indeed, in *Mame,* Miller's star was as polished as it ever was in Hollywood.

Miller is a sensational actress and she single-handedly kept the production running on Broadway for nearly another year, including a transfer across the street to the Broadway Theatre. "I had to leave the show when I got pneumonia," Miller remembers. "It was kind of a heartbreak, but to this day I'm grateful to John Bowab who originally saw me in *Can Can* in Texas and then put me in *Mame* in Florida."

Mame ultimately had a five-year run on Broadway, and hasn't stopped in 30-plus years, which led Jerry Herman to quip to the playwrights, "My God, this could be played by rabbits!"

Broadway star Carole Cook is perhaps the only actress to perform the role of Mame Dennis in both the comedy play *Auntie Mame* and the stage musical *Mame.* (Photo courtesy of Carole Cook)

Musical comedy star Jo Anne Worley has starred as Mame Dennis in multiple productions of *Mame.* (Photo courtesy of Jo Anne Worley)

Jane A. Johnston starred as the sodden Vera Charles in a critically acclaimed performance of *Mame.* (Photo courtesy of Jane A. Johnston)

CHAPTER EIGHT

Mame: The Movie Musical

AS THE "FLOWER POWER" 1960s dissolved into the 1970s, Hollywood and its marketing of increasingly provocative material was rattling the sensibilities of more than just a few Right Wing Fundamentalists. Submitting to pressure from the National Catholic Office for Motion Pictures and various civic coalitions, the film industry instituted a movie rating system in 1968. Designed to advise patrons of a film's content *before* they paid their money at the box office, it was determined that a review panel would screen all films before theatrical distribution of a movie, and assign a stamp of endorsement: G – General Audiences, appropriate for all ages; M – Suggested for mature audiences; R – Restricted, persons under 16 not admitted, unless accompanied by parent or legal guardian; and X – Explicit sexual content, no one under 21 admitted.

Lucille Ball was among the staunch advocates of these newly instituted film guidelines. In the early 1970s, she championed it as Hollywood's *duty* to create more wholesome features. "There are too many lines around the wrong movie houses these days," she barked, in reference to the growing number of sexually-explicit motion pictures increasingly offered to the general public. She took special vitriolic aim at the French-Italian film *Last Tango in Paris* directed by internationally respected filmmaker Bernardo Bertolucci.

Considered the most controversial film of its time, in Lucy's blue eyes *Last Tango* was a paradigm of what was wrong with the industry. "I don't know why Marlon Brando would lower himself to do a film like that," she thundered, with contempt for one of the actor's most acclaimed performances. "I think there are a lot of dirty old men out there making a fast buck and confusing young people. I'm beginning to be shocked that I'm not as shocked as I used to be," she cracked.

"Lucy wasn't a prude," notes Thomas J. Watson, the star's personal assistant, "but she believed that entertainment and entertainers had a certain responsibility to put a little hope into the world. Lucy liked to be involved in projects that had a positive re-enforcing effect on life. She didn't believe that movies and television necessarily needed to be an open window to the world, but she also didn't want to preach. Lucy believed what her first boss, Sam Goldwyn, said: 'If you want to send a message, call Western Union.'"

When it was announced in the showbiz trade paper *Daily Variety* on July 13, 1970, that *Mame* – certainly entertainment suitable for all ages – would finally be made into a motion picture, Lucy arched a knowing eyebrow. Having twice witnessed Angela Lansbury's triumph when it came West to Los Angeles' Dorothy Chandler Pavilion, Lucy saw this as an ideal vehicle to entertain what she felt was a neglected mass audience of people who had stopped patronizing films because the product was increasingly distasteful, if not bordering on the pornographic.

Several years earlier, when *Hello, Dolly!* was going into production, Ball was one of the earliest contenders for the title role. Much like *Mame*, many showbiz legends desperately wanted the film role of Dolly Levi. Ultimately, 20th Century-Fox selected Barbra Streisand – even before filming began on *Funny Girl*. Too young for the role, Streisand nevertheless got the studio's blessing. As one wag exclaimed, "There she was, all of 26, singing 'Before the Parade Passes By.'" Streisand won the coveted role because the studio wanted someone who would guarantee box office business. This was precisely the case in casting the lead for *Mame*.

Despite what show business publicists would have the world believe, Hollywood has always been a place where talent takes a back seat to the bottom line potential profits. For a then-staggering $3 million, said to be second only (up to that time) to the $5.5 million paid for *My Fair Lady* for screen rights, Warner Bros. and the American Broadcasting Company co-purchased the motion picture rights to *Mame* and they were determined that a "superstar" with the magic touch of Streisand would be cast for the choice role; not just a relatively (to them) insignificant Broadway actress with a diminutive (next to their Oscar) Tony Award to her credit.

One giant who loomed immediately in their collective consciousness even had a built-in cult of 42 million television viewers tuning in each week to catch her wacky situation comedy, *I Love Lucy*, and its subsequent incarnations.

From a marketing standpoint, the high-rated and universally beloved redhead, Lucille Ball, appeared to be the only logical candidate for the role. Never mind that the clever clown perhaps lacked the particular elegance and sophistication required of Patrick Dennis' eccentric aunt, or even that she wasn't a singer or dancer, as the star herself freely admitted. She had what was called a "Q" rating (awareness level among television viewers) of 98 – perhaps the highest of anyone in the world.

After 22 years of being a prime-time icon on the small screen, Lucille Ball was eager to return to motion pictures where she had begun as a "Goldwyn Girl" in 1933. To Ball, raised in Hollywood's Golden Age, being a star meant being a "movie star" – despite her unparalleled television success. And when she was offered the prized role of Mame, she seized the opportunity.

"Angela would have been perfect for the role," insists

playwright Jerome Lawrence. "Bette Davis wanted to do Vera and we wanted Carol Burnett for Gooch. That would have been such a classic cast."

But why wasn't Lansbury selected for the role that she created

Tony Award winners Frankie Michaels as young Patrick Dennis, and Angela Lansbury as Mame Dennis in the 1966 musical *Mame*. (Courtesy of Jerome Lawrence).

185

and for which she received stunning praise? The answer, quite simply, was money. Warner Bros. executives did not feel that Angela Lansbury was a big enough star to carry such an expensive motion picture. Even though she had two Tony Awards and three Oscar nominations to her credit – and had been in movies since 1944 – Lansbury still wasn't considered a big enough name.

The financial wizards at Warner Bros. obviously did not feel that Lansbury would attract their target audience. Prior to her hit television series *Murder, She Wrote*, Lansbury's following had been primarily in the big theatre cities. She had never carried a successful film on the strength of her own name, and the feeling was that this film's success would be severely compromised if Lansbury was cast in the lead. So they enticed Lucille Ball to accept the role.

But it was nevertheless still uncertain if Lucy's legion of admirers would leave the comfort of their respective couches and Lay-Z-Boy recliners, to pay to see their beloved Monday-night TV fixture at a movie theatre. And, equally important, would the world still love Lucy *after Mame*? This was a gamble that the so-called "experts" in charge at Warner Bros. were willing to take, and, for her part, Lucy was anxious to see if her legions of television fans would accept her in a character other than her scatterbrained "Lucy" small-screen persona in the increasingly old-fashioned genre known as the *movie musical*.

When it was announced in 1972 that *Mame* would indeed be filmed with Lucille Ball in the title role, many in the entertainment industry were stunned – much as they were when the voice of God rang out, "Rosalind Russell shall hitherto be known as Mama Rose," as Russell absconded with the role that most everyone thought was rightfully Ethel Merman's in the film version of "Gypsy." To many, it was practically an irreverent desecration, and inconceivable that anyone other that Angela Lansbury should have the screen role of Mame Dennis.

Author Patrick Dennis flatly said, "Miss Ball is a good comedienne, but a little too common for the role. However, it has by now been played by so many women that it really doesn't make much difference."

Despite maintaining an attitude of graciousness, Lansbury was understandably devastated in losing the role to Ball. "I wanted to make the film of *Mame* in the worst way," she revealed in an interview at the time. (Regarding Lansbury's quote, an amusing letter to the Los Angeles *Times*, said, "Isn't it interesting that Ms. Lansbury said she wanted to make a film of *Mame* in the worst way, and that is exactly the way Lucille Ball did it.")

"But I was, quite simply, never asked." Lansubry continued. "By the way, did anyone ask Julie Andrews to do *My Fair Lady*? Look, I think Lucy was in a position to be offered the part, and I think she ran with the ball – no pun intended. I don't blame Lucy a bit. I'd have done the same thing. And she's got Beatrice Arthur, one of the most skillful, funny women who ever tottered on two feet."

But Lansbury confessed to intimates that after being snubbed by Hollywood for the role she made famous, she did wince whenever she saw the larger-than-life billboards of Lucy with a long cigarette holder clenched between her teeth advertising the motion picture. "I think she plays Auntie Mame. I played Mame Dennis," Lansbury astutely noted. "Of course, I like to think I have a little more warmth," she added, "but I have no doubt it will be a success and people who haven't been out in years will leave their television sets to see Lucy in the movies."

Yet, as Lucille Ball confidant Thomas Watson offers, "Lucy was always trying to downplay the fact that she stole the part from Angela. Indeed, she did *not* go after the role; they came to her because she was a universally recognized name. Warner Bros. didn't think anyone in Iowa would know, or even care, who Angela Lansbury was."

However, in 1974, when author James Gregory interviewed Lucy during the filming of *Mame* for his book, *The Lucille Ball Story*, he quoted the star insisting that Lansbury had no interest in doing the film. "I loved Angela in [the Broadway musical] so much that I spent *months* trying to talk people into having *her* do it. But *she* turned it down! She took off for Ireland or something, and didn't want any part of it. She felt she'd given all that she could."

According to Watson, Lucy agreed to do the motion picture version of *Mame* because she knew her television series was winding down (ending in the spring of 1974), and wanted to open new creative avenues for herself. She, in fact, hadn't been in a feature film since 1968's *Yours Mine and Ours* with Henry Fonda.

With a two-picture deal at Warner Bros., producer Robert Fryer (with James Cresson) was once again at the helm of yet another vehicle featuring his precious Mame character, making this the fourth incarnation of Patrick Dennis' fictional aunt that he was involved with.

Pulitzer Prize-winning playwright Paul Zindel (*The Effect of Gamma Rays on Man-in-the-Moon Marigolds*) was asked to meet with the producers and Lucille Ball to discuss his writing the film adaptation of the Broadway musical.

Zindel had just completed the script for Barbra Streisand's feature *Up the Sandbox* when he received a call from his agent at the William Morris office instructing him to immediately go to the Ball residence at 1000 North Roxbury Drive in Beverly Hills to discuss with the star his possible participation in *Mame*. He was delighted. "Let's face it," he says, "the assignment was a plum. Only a curmudgeon wouldn't want to do it.

"I was a chemistry teacher who had just left teaching at a high school in Staten Island in 1968," the dramatist continues. "So I went very excitedly – and unknowingly – toward the *Mame* project."

It was an awkward, tortuous first meeting for Zindel. He had been approved as screenwriter by the producers and the studio, but he had to face one final test before signing a contract – he had to meet with and be endorsed by the star. Zindel's understandable nervousness was augmented to terror because actor/director Charles Nelson Reilly had alerted him that Lucille Ball was a very tough lady and nothing like her wacky, lovable television persona. Zindel didn't know what to expect.

"I arrived at Lucy's house, walked up to the door, rang the bell, and to my shock, she answered the door herself," Zindel recalls of that initial meeting. "She was very down to earth and absolutely nice to me in her own way, but I was terrified because I couldn't get an immediate rapport with her," he says.

Zindel spent the next five hours at Lucy's home trying to forge a bond with the star. It was only after watching three hours of excerpts from her TV series and dining at Matteo's in Beverly Hills that she finally began to warm to him.

Ball was, as he had expected, a brittle, opinionated woman who adamantly declared that if she was to become involved in this film project, one of the things she wanted to do was to "preserve the integrity" of the Broadway musical in the movie adaptation. Yet, despite her stand against vulgarity, she even insisted on speaking the line "Life is a banquet but most poor sons-of-bitches are starving to death!" (Unfortunately, the studio made her record three watered-down versions, ultimately using "most poor *slobs*…" for the film's television version.)

Lucy was shrewd enough to insist on surrounding herself with as many people from the original Broadway production of *Mame* as possible. "I had cast approval and corrected a couple of mistakes that had been made originally," the star once said. One of the "mistakes" was the suggestion that Rock Hudson play Beauregard, to which Lucy flatly refused. The studio felt that his presence would help attract an audience, but she remained steadfast in her veto, although she had enjoyed working with him on one of her early TV episodes. The star's superb choice for the role was Robert Preston, whom Ball had greatly admired since seeing him in *The Music Man*.

In addition to requesting Tony Award-winner Beatrice Arthur to recreate her role as Vera Charles, Ball also insisted on hiring legendary choreographer Onna White. White – who was presented with an Academy Award for her choreography in *Oliver!* in 1968 – was known to be a rigorous authoritarian when it came to dance and discipline. She was wary about working with the difficult, demanding Ball, but agreed to meet with Lucy to discuss the project.

White went to Lucy's house in Beverly Hills, and she quite sternly informed the case-hardened star – in no uncertain terms that dancing in *Mame* would require a great deal of hard work and stamina.

"Miss Ball," White demanded, "if you think this is going to be easy, you're totally mistaken. I don't care what anyone tells you, this is not an easy role."

In recalling that first meeting, White offers, "I learned right away that you had to tell Lucy what to do. You didn't ask Lucy what she would like to do. You told her what you wanted her to do."

Lucy was noticeably limping after breaking her right leg less than a year earlier while skiing in Aspen during a family vacation. While Onna White was compassionate she nevertheless

In 1974, America's favorite comedienne, Lucille Ball, starred in the film adaptation of the Tony Award-winning Broadway musical, *Mame.*

told her, "I want you to know that you have to buckle down because I'm going to give you a lot of hard work to do." As formidable as White appeared to be, she was just the type of personality that Lucy respected and would work hard to please.

Recalling the first day of rehearsal at The Burbank Studios, White says, "Lucy came in that morning with a steel brace on her leg. I said to the chauffeur, 'Take that off! I never want to see that thing again!'

"Lucy was protecting herself in case she wasn't good enough.

Academy Award winning choreographer Onna White (right) puts Lucille Ball (left) through a rigorous dance rehearsal for the motion picture adaptation of the musical, *Mame*. ©1974 Warner Bros. Inc. All rights Reserved.

I know how these stars are. I insisted that Lucy get herself over to the barre in the gymnasium. I gave her special exercises to strengthen her leg and that was the end of it. She worked very hard and danced quite well for me out in the potholes at the Disney Ranch where we filmed the fox hunt scene. And when Lucy's doctor took a last examination of her leg, he said, 'The woman who cured your leg deserves a medal!'"

Rehearsals began in August, 1972, at the Burbank Warner Bros. Studio. At the first script read-through Ball immediately began her battle of will against anyone who challenged her – without good reason. Screenwriter Zindel says that despite Lucy's feelings to the contrary, the studio decided they still wanted a few fresh things in the movie, a few nuances to make it a bit different from the stage show. One item was a new song by Jerry Herman – "Loving You" to be sung by Beauregard – and the other was the studio wanted a new actress to play Agnes Gooch, instead of casting from the stage production.

"Apparently they cast Madeline Kahn as Gooch without clearing it with Lucy, or not listening to her grumblings," Zindel reveals. "The first time Lucy and Madeline met was at the very first rehearsal. They began to read and as Madeline spoke her first line, Lucy interrupted and abruptly said to her, 'Listen, what kind of voice are you going to use in this?' Madeline patiently said, 'What do you mean what kind of voice am I going to use?' To which Lucy responded curtly, 'Well, you've got to use a trick voice here, why don't you start using it right now. Let me hear the voice.'

"There was silence in the rehearsal room as Madeline coldly stated, 'I will arrive at the voice *after* some rehearsal and building of the character.'

"Lucille Ball affirmed, 'Oh no. You use the voice *now!*'

"That was the end of Madeline Kahn in *Mame*," Zindel says.

"She was out of there that day."

"I'm not exactly sure what happened," Kahn told Rex Reed in the author's book *Valentines & Vitriol.* "They showed Lucille Ball *What's Up, Doc?* and she liked me in it, but then I walked on the set and I guess I don't exactly look like frumpy Enunice from the movie. It was just a part. I mean, you can see I don't look like that in real life. But I thought that was what the movies were about. Hey, nobody walks around Hollywood looking the way they really look. I can look like forty different people with makeup and padding. I didn't think it was a problem, but I think when Lucille Ball met me, she thought, 'What kind of casting is this?' And I must admit I'm no Agnes Gooch. But I planned to play it differently from the way Jane Connell played it on Broadway and I thought they wanted a different approach too. The problem was do we go in a new direction or do we do what's already been done? They got Jane Connell and there's your answer. But I didn't take it as a personal insult or pesonal rejection. That's just show business."

As Thomas Watson notes, "Lucy was *always* a director. She

Jane Connell, portrayed Gooch in the Broadway and Hollywood musicals, *Mame.*

had her opinions on everything and got her own way even when it was to her detriment. Madeline and Lucy's personalities were like oil and water. Lucy wanted her to play Gooch. She did not want any of Madeline Kahn's personality showing through. Lucy insisted that Madeline subordinate some of her own comedy in order to play the role as written."

Laugh-In comedienne Ruth Buzzi, was tested to replace Kahn but Jane Connell, who had performed the part on Broadway, ultimately took over. "I think the new breed of comedienne confused Lucy," Connell says. "Also I suspect that she felt a little threatened by Madeline's youth at the time. So she told Gene Saks, 'Get me the Gooch I saw at the Dorothy Chandler Pavilion!'"

Connell won the role after a screen test and although the long production period became a very positive experience for her, she arrived on the set in Burbank ready to deal with just about anything. "Madeline Kahn was dearly loved and I was going into a situation where I was the star's pet because I was her choice," Connell reflects. "I think Lucy felt ganged up on, in a way."

The Madeline Kahn saga wasn't the only casting snag that occurred in the initial stages of rehearsal. On December 22, 1972, The *Hollywood Reporter* announced that co-star Beatrice Arthur had quit because of conceptual differences with Miss Ball over Arthur's handling of the part she created on Broadway, and that Bette Davis had been asked to take over for her.

"Lucy always denied that rumor," says Thomas Watson. "Beatrice and Lucy were always friends. She said that of all the erroneous things that had been written about her over the years she never cared to sue anybody because it doubles the problem."

However, the angry star announced she was seriously considering suing the paper, and a hasty retraction appeared in The *Hollywood Reporter* the next day.

Yet, according to more than a few observers, there appears to be at least a kernel of truth to the rumor about personal differences between the two ladies.

"Lucy was very camera-wise," notes Watson. "She had been in the business for 40 years and knew that if you had green nail polish on in one scene, you jolly well better have it on in the next scene if the two were to be cut together. Beatrice didn't like the idea that Lucy thought she knew more about Vera Charles than she did. Beatrice felt, why should I wear nail polish if they aren't going to see my hands. It was just a difference in the two ladies' styles," Watson says. "But it never got dirty."

The location shooting at the Disney Ranch proved an arduous as well as a potentially hazardous locale – especially for Lucy and the dancers. Onna White recalls that there were a lot of rattlesnakes in the area and that the crew would arrive at the location early in the morning just to look for and remove rattlers.

In addition to snakes, gopher holes were everywhere. White remembers that "in the middle of one scene, Lucy screamed, 'Stop! Stop everything! There's a gopher hole! I want it filled! I want all the gopher holes on this property filled before tomorrow.

"Bosom Buddies" Vera Charles (Beatrice Arthur, left) and Mame Dennis (Lucille Ball, right), in Warner Bros. musical, *Mame.* ©1974 Warner Bros. Inc. All rights Reserved.

Is that *clear!*' She just didn't want the dancers to hurt themselves," White says in defense of the star's tantrum.

It was a grueling schedule for the 62-year-old star. As the queen of television comedy she never had to be up before 8:00 a.m. to do her weekly show. Lucy would arrive at the studio at 10:00 a.m., four days a week, and be home by 5:30 each afternoon, except the night of filming. However, for the 92 days of shooting *Mame*, Lucy got up at 5:00 a.m., six days a week. But if she thought *filming Mame* was difficult, she would later learn that *living* with *Mame* was even more upsetting, if not downright devastating.

Mame completed principal photography at The Burbank Studios on June 5, 1973, just in time to prepare the film for its anticipated Christmas week opening. Generally considered the most prestigious and one of the most profitable times to release a film – openings toward the end of the year are also most fresh in the memory of the Motion Picture Academy members when Oscar nominations are determined in February. And a big budget musical like *Mame* seemed a cinch to garner all sorts of nominations and awards.

But this was not to be. While Lucy was on the set of her comedy series, editor Maury Winetrobe tackled the film footage of *Mame*, bleary-eyed, trying to assemble an acceptable first cut. It was an especially arduous task because contractually they could not cut or pare down any of the songs.

After several months of post-production work, the studio was forced to announce that *Mame* would not be released as originally planned but would instead be held until the Easter 1974 season. The Hollywood rumor mill began churning, dredging up all sorts of fertile mulch as to why the film's release was being postponed. In defense of the picture and to quell negative speculation, producer Robert Fryer innocently said in print, "We just want to be able to sell this picture properly. Besides, too many films come out at Christmas."

To insiders, however, it was obvious that the studio sensed they had less than what they had hoped for in the way of a big, splashy, old-fashioned but glamorously entertaining musical.

Hollywood legend has dictated that hype can work wonders for a mediocre property, and the Warner Bros. publicity machine accelerated its advance hoopla for *Mame*. They let it be known as far and wide as possible that the world would soon be surprised by the depth of Lucille Ball's acting ability. They injected newsy bits to the effect that although the public had known for years that Lucy could make them laugh, watch out because they were in for a delightful surprise at her touching, warm performance in the film.

Typical of her generation of film stars, groomed by the "studio system," Lucy believed that making a movie was only half of her job as an actress, that she was obligated to the project and to go out and "sell" it, and readily agreed to a strenuous global tour to promote the film. To launch the proceedings a huge premiere was arranged at the Pacific Theatres Cinerama Dome on Sunset Boulevard in Los Angeles.

The Hollywood premiere was one of the most dazzling in the town's history of spectacular openings. Being Easter, a giant colorful bonnet crowned the distinctive geometric dome of the famous circular theatre. The bonnet, designed by the film's costume designer, Theodora Van Runkle, measured 550 feet at its circumference and 175 feet in diameter, and used ten thousand feet of hat material. The bow in front was 50 feet wide, and the two-foot lace around its brim stretched 300 feet.

In addition to touting the musical motion picture *Mame*, the evening was a benefit sponsoring the Opera Guild of Southern California. Hundreds of invited guests arrived in vintage automobiles, wearing period costumes of the 1920s. Stepping out onto red carpets dividing the motion picture elite and hundreds of star-struck spectators, Lucille Ball emerged from a 1910 Packard limousine, draped in an all-white furry costume from the film. Thousands of tiny bubbles arched over Sunset Boulevard as a 250-piece band marched under the direction of Marvin Marker; the Long Beach Junior Concert Band and Color Guard provided a musical salute; and *Daily Variety* columnist Army Archerd announced the arrival of each V.I.P., as formally gowned usherettes wearing corsages of spring flowers assisted the invited guests in finding their reserved seats.

Surrounded by friends, colleagues and business associates who under the circumstances had little choice but to praise Lucy's performance at the post screening party – Lucy was unprepared for the blistering critical attacks that soon came – an irrevocable blow to her career, from which she never fully recovered.

It seems that Angela Lansbury's performance in *Mame* was rather a sacred cow to the critics, and where *Mame* was concerned, they were still petulant that she had been bypassed in favor of clown Lucy for the motion picture version of this hit Broadway show. The hatchet men at the big city papers were sharpening their implements of justice, eagerly waiting for *Mame* to be released and to pounce on Lucille Ball with their hostile judgments.

When the motion picture officially opened on March 27, 1974, the negative, and often unsparingly cruel, reviews implied that Lucille Ball had lost her talents, judgment and beauty – the desperate attempt to hide Ball's aging appearance made all the more pathetic by extensive soft-focus lenses and lighting was a jarring contrast to shots not including Ball. The media was almost unanimous in their arch disapproval of the star and her film.

Mary Knoblauch in her *Chicago Today* film column wrote: "If *Mame* is a smash, it will be television's final revenge on the movie world, for *Mame* is a travesty of the original story, which survived intact from novel to play to film to stage musical. This *Mame* is a geriatric love story in which Lucille Ball drops her nephew the moment she falls in love with Robert Preston, and ignores him as long as Preston is alive.

"*Mame* is not so much old fashioned as tawdry and inept. In the original story and a more truthful camera on the star, it might have been tolerable. But this futile and embarrassing attempt to change a character comedy into a middle-aged love story is disaster. When a film makes you embarrassed for its actors, there is something so basically wrong that you wonder why the makers couldn't see it."

But many of the so-called critics didn't stop with their condemnation of the usual elements of a bad picture (e.g. misdirection, poor dialogue, improper lighting, etc.), they took special, deadly aim at Lucy.

As Frank Rich of the *New York Times* announced, "The biggest turkey on Beekman Place is star Lucille Ball. To make matters worse, [Gene] Saks accommodates the elderly star's wrinkles by shooting her close-ups in soft focus – so gauzy you think you're in a hospital…"

"She is too thick in the waist, too stringy in the legs, too basso in the voice, and too creaky in the joints," concluded *The New Republic*.

"The sound is somewhere between a bark and a croak…and it doesn't quite match the movement of the lips," noted *The New Yorker*. "Did Lucille Ball sync her own singing in *Mame* or did Dick Cavett dub for her? After more than 40 years in movies and television, did she discover in herself an unfulfilled ambition to be a flaming drag queen?"

"There she stands, her aging face practically a blur in the protective gauze of softer than soft focus…looking alternately like any one of the seven deadly sins…" reported *Newsweek* magazine.

"'Who charmed the husks right off the corn?' No Virginia, it's not Mame – it's Lucille Ball who picked it and leaves it flopping around like a dying perch stuck between the vaselined lens and supreme ego of the actress," jeered critic David Galligan of the show business industry trade paper *Drama-Logue*. "Miss Ball has managed to destroy the indestructible Auntie Mame." His final vitriolic judgment being: "Like the song says, 'She'll make the South revive again.' Unfortunately, it will probably be to *lynch* Lucy."

Lucille Ball was, understandably, completely devastated.

On the Georgia plantation set of the film musical *Mame,* Lucille Ball as Mame Dennis and Robert Preston as Beauregard Jackson Pickett Burnside, rehearse a scene.

With nearly all the major critics wondering aloud and in print why she would even consider doing a film that called for a much younger (15 years or more) singer/dancer, and the obvious, unsuccessful pains it took to carefully photograph her to disguise her age, the star crumbled. There were rumors that the tab just for retouching publicity stills of the actress went into five figures. And, it was reported that when critic Gene Siskel of the *Chicago Tribune* arrived to interview her at the star's hotel suite in New York where she was staying during her East Coast publicity tour, she broke down and began sobbing.

"It's not that I'm tired," she cried, tears rolling down her face. "It's the pictures they've taken and what they've written about me. The studio spent plenty of money to get the best photographs of me in *Mame,* so why do the newspapers have to send people just so they can take ugly pictures of me? So I look my age. What's wrong with that? These stories make me feel wrong and old," she weeped. "I would think these journalists would like to keep the entertainment business alive, but with this kind of stuff, they're killing it!"

Lucy was demolished by the reviews. "She didn't expect them," says Thomas Watson. "When she saw *Mame* at a preview, it was 99% the way she wanted it. She didn't necessarily trust that it was a great movie by 1974 standards, but she had the attitude that 'if it's good enough for my mother, it's good enough for me.'"

Lucy elaborated on that statement when she appeared on one of Phil Donahue's early shows from his original outlet in Cleveland. When asked by the host why she would want to make a movie like *Mame* at this stage in her career, Lucy looked at her audience of mostly housewives and said, "I did it for these ladies. I wanted to make a woman's picture, the way we used to do at MGM. I wanted something that the average housewife could go out and see and feel good about."

But in the 1970s, housewives weren't the primary movie-going audience. As is the case today, motion pictures were essentially a medium that attracted younger patrons. Lucy wanted *Mame* to be a glossy, escapist, women-oriented musical.

In television, until her ill-fated last series in 1986, Lucy was revered, regarded no less than an American institution. Critics may have disliked her shows, but they invariably loved the red-head. She was used to people saying that her shows were trivial but that the lady is wonderful, that her presence and magic made the scripts work. It was a complete shock for the 62-year-old legend to have the critics snipe, "This lady has turned a Broadway masterpiece into a dud."

Until her death in 1989, Lucille Ball couldn't comprehend why *Mame* failed as a motion picture, other than acknowledging that the audience it was targeted for perhaps no longer existed. She pondered the fact that other stars such as Bette Davis had made many movies past their prime, and yet they were not written off so quickly by personal and critical vendettas.

She also blamed the Warner Bros. publicity department for not promoting the film properly. Lucy believed that when they realized the potential for other films, they put nine-tenths of their time and energy into publicizing those instead of her *Mame*. She failed to accept the possibility that her own brittle, unappealing performance perhaps lacking in warmth, color and substance, contributed to the film's failure.

Obviously, producing a motion picture musical based on the hit Broadway stage musical *Mame* may have been a bigger gamble than anyone anticipated. Audiences were not going to see those kinds of movies anymore and studios, for the most part, were not bankrolling musicals.

The box office failure of *Mame* was really the end of a long string of motion picture musicals that had flopped one after another, including *Dr. Dolittle, Star!, Darling Lili* and *Paint Your Wagon*. By the time the 1970s rolled around that genre was practically dead.

"Instead of *My Fair Lady* being the start of a revival of the movie musical," notes showbusiness historian Thomas Watson, "I think they were just lucky. *Mary Poppins* and *The Sound of Music* were practically the only successful musicals since the mid-1950s. They were the exception to the fact that the musical format doesn't work anymore. Then some idiot said, 'Oh, musicals are back.' And they bombed."

It would have been an uphill battle to succeed with *Mame* no matter who the studio had cast in the title role. People – particularly younger moviegoers – were unable to accept screen characters bursting into song for no dramatic reason. In retrospect, if one rules out Angela Lansbury, as Warner Bros. did; and you purge Lucille Ball, as the critics did, who would have been a viable alternative in 1974? *Mame* was just the last in a long line of expensive, lavish, disappointments.

But, despite the negative reviews of *Mame,* the film did break several house records when it debuted with the Rockettes for the annual Easter show at Radio City Music Hall in New York. By May 17, 1974, it was announced in the *Hollywood Reporter* that *Mame* had set box office records and hit a total gross of $2,707,097 during its 10-week world premiere engagement at Radio City. According to press releses the records included the all-time one-week highest gross for one theatre of $402,244 (set during its sixth week); and the highest single day's business in history for any film theatre with $69,220 recorded Saturday, March 23, during its final week.

Reflecting today on the failure of the motion picture *Mame,* composer Jerry Herman candidly admits, "Warner Bros. wanted a box office star, and anytime a motion picture company says they want a box office star for a film, and the star is wrong for the property, they end up with what happened with the motion picture of *Mame.*

"Nobody admired Lucille Ball more than I," he continues. "She was a great lady and a very hard worker. But she was simply not right for the role. A clown cannot play that part and we had America's greatest clown. Mame is a Greer Garson, an elegant lady. When she does something that's a little crazy, the audience is delighted. If Queen Elizabeth did something a little off-color, it would be twice as funny than if Phyllis Diller did the same thing, because we know that Queen Elizabeth is a great lady."

By the time *Mame* was released audiences had been programmed to think of Lucy as "Lucy Ricardo," not as a poised society woman, unless it was meant to be a befuddled society matron in the tradition of Margaret Dumont as foil for the antics of the Marx brothers. Ball wound up pleasing no one because the New York sophisticates who wanted Angela Lansbury wrote Lucy off before she even started, and her television fans were disappointed because they demanded the baggy-pants small-screen "Lucy." In the end, the movie appealed to very few.

"She believed it was the best she could have done," says Thomas Watson. "If she were alive today and they gave her the money to make it again, I don't know that she would know what to change, except tightening it up a little and making it less lavish." In fact, according to Watson, Lucy owned a 35mm uncut print of the film which she later enjoyed screening in her home projection room.

"I'm not saying that *Mame* will be a re-discovered classic twenty years from now," Watson concludes. "I just don't think it's as bad as some people thought it was when it was first released. Its worst sin was not being in the spirit of the time it was made. It would have been great in 1948. If you look at it in that regard, I don't think the movie is bad, just flawed."

Paul Zindel agrees: "I think in the long run, the movie will end up being what it was intended to be, the consummate movie enshrinement of Lucille Ball."

And if the property hadn't been so indestructible, Lucille Ball might have ruined *Mame* forever.

CHAPTER NINE

The Real Auntie Mame

"Is *AUNTIE MAME* authentic biography?" queried book reviewer Ben Crisler, in the January 23, 1955, Sunday edition of the New York *Times*. "The possibility is alarming," he declared. "Yet, except for a few obviously hoaxed-up passages the whole thing seems far too improbable to be merely fictional."

While it was publicly stated in print – even in show business trade papers – that Auntie Mame was *really* actress Gertrude Lawrence, and that author Patrick Dennis was *actually* a writer named Virginia Rowans, who "knew" Miss Lawrence, Dennis, remained adamant throughout his life. "*Auntie Mame* is not, repeat, not autobiographical," he said. "While I've known a great many eccentric people like Mame, she is a distillation and a moonbeam and nothing more!"

To the contrary, Marion Tanner, the author's aunt, insisted until her death in 1985 that indeed there was one real-life model and inspiration for her nephew's famous character – and that she *was* that person. Interestingly enough, Marion died October 31, exactly 19 years to the day that *Auntie Mame* opened on Broadway.

Harvest Years magazine profiled Marion in 1970 as "The Real Auntie Mame," and though Marion Tanner was eccentric – she was once paid five dollars to jump off a cliff for a *Perils of Pauline* serial – she was more a humanitarian than an avant-garde social revolutionary. She earned a master's degree in sociology from Smith College, and for 35 years opened her four-story brownstone house at 72 Bank Street in New York to any number or variety of artists and transients – "visitors" as she referred to them. According to her friend Frank Andrews, "She took the locks off the front door and taped a sign handwritten in pencil over the doorbell that read: 'A Home for Wayward Uncles and Aunts.'"

"Somehow *Auntie Mame* sounds awfully real," agreed Margaret Parton in her review of the book in the *New York Herald Tribune*. "And the fact that Mr. Dennis has chosen to use a pseudonym only bolsters the suspicion that there really is a lady like Mame. Anyway, we hope so."

But Marion Tanner was also described as rather a thorn in Patrick Dennis' side. "The woman was publicity mad," revealed one acquaintance. "The fact that Marion proclaimed herself the original Auntie Mame annoyed Pat to no end."

Dennis even once fumed, "The only resemblance between Auntie Mame and my Aunt Marion is that my Aunt Marion is indeed mad!"

"Obviously," Marion declared in defense of her claim to fame, "he [Patrick Dennis] glamorized everything."

In her own way, however, Marion was equally as interesting as the fictional Mame Dennis Burnside. In her younger years she was an actress with the renowned Castle Hill Players, of which Alfred Lunt was a juvenile player. She appeared as "Granny" in an off-Broadway revival of *Tobacco Road* and had the female lead in a low budget film entitled *The Auto Bandits of New York*.

As she grew older – and her income diminished – Marion transformed her beautiful old Georgian-style house located on Bank Street into small apartments, renting flats to an endless procession of creative and theatrical people.

Actress/painter Marguerite Lewis, who appeared in such Broadway stage productions as *The House in Paris* (1944), *Marriage Is for Single People* (1945) and the 1949 Hume Cronyndirected play *Now I Lay Me Down to Sleep* starring Fredrick March and Florence Eldridge, says of her early days living at the renowned 72 Bank Street with Marion Tanner: "It was a very colorful place to be when I lived there. It was totally Bohemian. I was an aspiring actress, and took the flat that Miriam Hopkins once lived in. In another flat lived the writer Harry Brown, who wrote *A Walk in the Sun*.

"Although Marion was rather dowdy in appearance – she had short-cropped iron-gray hair, wore lisle stockings, cardigans and skirts and looked rather frumpy – she was always feeding somebody. No one ever went hungry in Marion's household, even if she only had a squash to share with you, she would make certain you had something to eat. She was filled with loving kindness, but didn't have a lot of horse sense. She was a great windmill tilter."

Lewis remembers Marion Tanner as a very charismatic woman. "She couldn't have been a kinder, sweeter woman but she was also a total bubble head. She was a totally quixotic human being. But she was very lovable and had the most marvelous big brown eyes, the sweetest smile and a heart as big as Bank Street. She was certainly a woman born 50 years ahead of her time. She was a character, and a darling woman."

Unfortunately, in later years, Marion let the mortgage payments on her house lapse. Though many friends and former "visitors" contributed money on her behalf, most of the funds collected went to pay her back income taxes and for food for her tenants. After much publicity and several temporary reprieves, Marion was finally evicted in July 1964.

"She was in a state of shock," remembers Frank Andrews of the dire situation in which Tanner found herself. "She did not believe this was going to happen. We had heated discussions before the foreclosure and Marion said to me, 'God will provide.'

Well, God didn't provide. The Marshal came and evicted everyone from the place."

By this time, according to Andrews, the transients living at the Bank Street house were no longer the artists, writers and the colorful people Tanner had once accepted into her home such as actor Will Geer and singer Billie Holliday. Now, they were derelicts and Bowery bums. They stole from her. Unwed mothers found their way to Marion's door and left their babies with her. When Tanner and her tenants were evicted they had to build a shanty town at Abbington Square where they all lived in cardboard boxes. After a week, the police came and pushed them on.

"Though I lost touch with her after that," Andrews continues, "I heard that during the last part of her life she ended up in front of the Herbert Bergof Studios begging for money from people as they were coming out. So she ended up as a bag lady in the end.

"The movie [*Auntie Mame*] made it like she lived happily ever after, and everything was taken care of," Andrews says. "But that's not true.

"Marion was really a good soul and really meant well," Andrews adds. "It was just that things got out of hand. The people she took in weren't who she thought they were. You cannot make irresponsible people responsible by giving them a bath, food and shelter; and that's what she was trying to do. It was heartbreaking, to see this wonderful woman with her head in the clouds – and no feet on the ground."

"I definitely think Marion was an armature for the character of Auntie Mame in which he [Patrick Dennis] made her into the glamorous person he wanted her to be," observes Marguerite Lewis. "Marion had no glamour of her own, let me assure you, although she had done glamorous things. There was a decidedly theatrical and interesting aura about her."

Lewis also holds that the name for Patrick Dennis's fictional character may well have been inspired by her own stepfather's mother, Mary Fargo Balliot, who was known to her friends in Buffalo, New York, as *Mame* Balliot.

Lewis recalls that her stepfather used to play tennis with Edward Tanner, Jr. (Pat Tanner's father) who was a tennis champion. The Tanners and Balliots were friends all their lives, what used to be affectionately called "kissing cousins." Hence, when referring to Mame Balliot, the Tanner children called her Auntie Mame.

*

Whether a character of fictitious or authentic origin, the Auntie Mame that we have come to know had a unique and unconventional persona, which appears to be a psychological defense designed to cover a multitude of personal insecurities. People such as Mame are often reckless and impulsive because they feel they have little or no alternative. Such behavioral aberrations are said to be survival techniques.

Patrick Dennis didn't indicate in either *Auntie Mame* (or its sequel *Around the World With Auntie Mame*) what incidents in Mame's early fictional life may have led to her unconventional development. Because of her intelligence and decorum – called upon when convenient – she was probably born to the wealth she flaunted. However, if she had been without financial independence it is likely that Mame would have lived as a very isolated and unhappy person, because she wouldn't have had the monetary resources to indulge her emotional needs and eccentricities.

Mame perhaps adopted her larger-than-life persona in order to avoid dealing with the more complex and subtle aspects of her personality. If it is true that "our friends make our statements," as

some analysts theorize, then Mame was making overt pro-
nouncements which were seemingly outrageous and controversial in order to attract friends who, in turn, were larger-than-life,
outrageous and respected.

From an objective observation, one would suspect that Mame
didn't think she was anything but a "party girl" compared to
the friends she truly admired. Her best friend and cohort, Vera
Charles, for instance, was a famous actress; and frequent suitor
Lindsay Woolsey was a successful book publisher. Mame surrounded herself with the rich and famous, the avant-garde and
the socially peculiar to add value to her shallow self-image – an
identity which she buried among the characters on her cocktail-
crush guest list.

The transition from bogus clown to a compassionate, loving
woman begins when she inherits her orphaned nephew,
Patrick. We then begin to uncover the substantial human being
in Mame that has made her the perfect literary, stage and cine-
ma heroine.

The fact that Mame is outrageous makes little difference to
the wondrous young mind of her nephew Patrick. To him, the
unexpected is expected. Patrick, an only child who saw his
wealthy widowed father – usually suffering a morning-after
hangover – only at breakfast time, and who was cared for by
Norah Muldoon, a salaried servant, was sheltered and had no
conventional comparison of what a "normal" home life should
be. Until he entered Mame's life, the child was raised in a very
limited "proper" universe.

On the other hand, it is Patrick's innocent influence that
enables Mame's character to develop. Initially, Mame seems to
lack conventional morals, caring little about anything except
having fun and living life to its fullest measure. But, as a result
of Patrick's naïve and unquestioned love and need for her,

Mame slowly begins to form values and a sense of self-worth and becomes less self-centered. When Patrick is unwillingly sent away to boarding school by his estate trustee, Mr. Babcock of the Knickerbocker Bank, we see that a devastated Mame has made – probably for the first time in her life – a genuine, profound, emotional connection to another person. When people form an emotional attachment such as this bonding, it places value on themselves as well. It can be very frightening when one has manipulated one's world as long as Mame had, to explore one's own nature and to conclude that it isn't necessary constantly to present a superficial facade in order to be accepted and loved.

As Mame continues to unfold and establish her sense of self-esteem, she creates the proper environment for a more mature love of a romantic nature. Enter Beauregard Jackson Pickett Burnside, her Southern knight-in-shining-armor.

Without lessening her personal strengths, Mame's flamboyance diminishes. With Beau, she now has someone solid to hold onto. Though her unusual dress remains somewhat the same, we no longer find her cavorting in an anti-establishment manner. Her personality now gives way to aristocratic ideals of story-book propriety, as though to the manner born.

Beau is a handsome, rich, Southern gentleman. To him, women are ladies and he treats them as such. It is a very affirming relationship for Mame. Because these traits and feelings are innate in Mame – and no longer blocked or resisted – she falls into the mode very comfortably.

On the surface, Beau seems not to be as strong a personality as Mame, but we discover that his power is derived from what he gives away *to* Mame. He provides her with a pedestal, and, therefore, he assumes the responsibilities of strength.

Patrick goes on to college and Mame's tower of fortitude,

Beau, dies from being kicked in the head by a horse (in the comedy play and motion picture he falls off the Matterhorn in Switzerland). But by this stage of her life, Mame has matured to become consciously aware of her own resilience and tenacity. Financially secure, she now only requires love, which has always been essential to her life. Mame finds love in several forms: the physical love she takes from Brian O'Bannion, a "spirited, spiritual Irishman" and co-author on a book collaboration with Mame; the maternal love she feels for Agnes Gooch, her myopic, pregnant out-of-wedlock secretary; and, of course, the purest, most complete love she shares with her devoted nephew Patrick.

Actress Rosalind Russell once said of the legendary character, "She is far too dedicated to sheer fun to linger over the finer points of morality. At times she is skating on thin ice, but the ice holds and Mame skids adroitly to safety. The girl can do no wrong. We begin to see why Auntie Mame has become one of America's favorite heroines. She dares to be herself. Seldom ladylike in her behavior, Mame remains ladylike down to her manicured toe nails. She is the sophisticated symbol of a whole era of nonsense. Judged by conventional standards, her propriety may be a shambles, but her heart never budges from where every heart ought to be."

"The play has a very concise and structured story," notes playwright Robert E. Lee. "In the first act young Patrick saves Mame from the trap of hedonism and the residue of the 1920s, and gives her a focus for her life. In the second act, the coin is flipped, and Mame saves Patrick from falling into the trap of Babbittry."

With so many seemingly contradictory facets to her personality, one must ask, who is Auntie Mame, really, and why does she appeal to such a large audience?

The playwriting team of Jerome Lawrence and Robert E. Lee concur that "There is something fiercely familiar about Auntie Mame. We all have, or wish we had a freewheeling aunt like her. Mame is the enemy of conformity, restriction, bigotry, intolerance, anything which places corsets on our minds and our soaring spirits."

"Few people realize that this is a comic portrait of the first feminist," says Lawrence. "She is a much more important person of fiction for this century than we realize at first glance. She was taking licenses and dares and personal challenges that women didn't get around to until the 1960s or 1970s. Though there were flappers and people who made bathtub gin in the 1920s, Mame was much more intellectually and culturally advanced than just the average fliberty gibbet."

Added Rosalind Russell, "Whether her author plucked her out of his own past or dreamed her up in this bright, glittering present makes little difference. The difference is that the world is a brighter, wiser place for her creation. Whether she ever existed before, she certainly exists now."

For his part, Patrick Dennis offered, "Auntie Mame, as I see her, isn't made of meat and bones and rules and conventions like the rest of us. She's a froth of whipped cream and champagne and day dreams and *Nuit de Noel* Perfume. She's as warm as a Bunsen burner and on occasion, frostier than dry ice. She can keep you seething for three hours while she dresses and finally appears so devastatingly attractive that you decide it was all worth the wait. So you see, she's not mortal at all."

Dennis also once said to friends, "Anybody who knows me knows who Auntie Mame really is..." Then he pointed to himself.

CHAPTER TEN

Patrick Dennis: Auntie Mame's Creator

HIS REAL NAME was Edward Everett Tanner III. Although that monicker was never recognized in literary circles, from the middle of the 1950s, and until the 1970s, Tanner was a celebrated novelist whose library of 16 outrageously humorous and insightful books sold in the millions of copies. He was the first novelist to have three books simultaneously on the New York *Times* best-sellers list.

Edward Tanner, however, was never linked to any of those books. Under a plethora of pseudonyms, the credit for writing such national best-sellers as *Auntie Mame, Around the World With Auntie Mame* and *Little Me*, was given to Patrick Dennis – a name he selected from the New York telephone directory. In addition, he published under such *nom de plumes* as Sarah Brooks and Virginia Rowans, and though Tanner reaped the financial rewards, he also avoided the notoriety that frequently accompanies enormous literary success. And this is just as he wanted it.

The son of a stockbroker, Tanner was born in Chicago, Illinois, on May 18, 1921. "I was born in the same hospital, in the same room and in the same bed as actress Cornelia Otis Skinner – but in different years," he once quipped.

Raised in a very conventional Presbyterian environment in Evanston, he was a precocious and amusing child, and from an early age displayed the voyeuristic proclivities that would serve him well as a future novelist. He loved sitting in his mother's parlor as an innocuous spectator during her bridge-club

Auntie Mame creator Patrick Dennis (aka Edward Everett Tanner III) (Photo by Cris Alexander)

parties, innocently petting the family chow, while absorbing the sights and sounds around him. He mentally filed away the gossip of the neighborhood ladies for future reference, to be recreated and embellished in his fertile imagination many years later. His future books would actually be narrated by just such a naïve individual as young Tanner appeared to be – a polite, basically normal young man with decent impulses who unwittingly wanders into a crazy situation but is a willing and fascinated spectator on the sidelines.

After graduating from Evanston Township High School, where he first began to write what he referred to as "doggerel" as a reporter and feature writer for the school paper *The Evanstonian* (his weekly humor column called "Judy" kept its name until 1961), Tanner enrolled in the Art Institute of Chicago, determined to become an artist. However, World War II erupted, and within a year he found himself overseas driving an ambulance for the American Field Service on the Arabian Peninsula, North Africa, Italy and France.

Twice wounded, Tanner completed his tour of duty and returned to the States. He moved to New York, intent on using his artistic talents as a set designer for the Broadway theatre. Instead, he went to work at Stebben's Hardware store in order to make enough money to support himself while seeking design jobs that lamentably, never materialized. Instead of embarking on a show business career, he segued into a position as an account executive for the Franklin Spier advertising agency, and then as advertising manager at Creative Age Press. He was subsequently hired at Columbia Educational Books where he began ghostwriting for other authors, including *There's a Fly in This Room* and *The Doctor Has a Baby* in which he assumed the personality of "Evelyn Barkin."

During this time he also began free-lance writing, contributing first to *Mademoiselle* magazine a short story entitled "I Didn't Make a Sorority." The editors asked him if he would mind them using a woman's name as the author. He did not, thus beginning his practice of using pseudonyms for his material. Several years later, when asked by his editor at Vanguard Press why he still used a fictitious identity, he explained, "If your name was Edward Everett Tanner III, what would *you* do?" As aristocratic as his name sounded, he felt it was too long. He wanted to use the name Benson Hedges after the popular cigarette, but was persuaded otherwise.

Through mutual friends, he met Louise Stickney, also an author. They married on December 30, 1948, and the union produced two children, Michael and Elizabeth.

It was while he was employed as promotion director at *Foreign Affairs* magazine that Tanner began working on *Auntie Mame*. "The writing of *Auntie Mame* went on for a couple of years," recalls Louise. "He did a lot of it at work. Though it probably took him about 90 days in actual time, when you're working on someone else's time, there are always interruptions – like doing the job you're paid to do. You might describe his *modus operandi* as ninety days, separated by watching wrestling and soap operas."

Auntie Mame was Tanner's third book (*Oh, What a Wonderful Wedding* and *House Party*, appeared in 1953 and 1954, respectively, under the pseudonym Virginia Rowans, a name derived from Virginia Rounds (a brand of cigarette that Tanner enjoyed) and the first of 12 books that he wrote under the pen name Patrick Dennis. Nineteen publishers rejected the novel in quick succession before Vanguard Press decided to take a chance with the unusual offering. "It's amazing how unfavorable readers' reports disappear from publishers files after a book becomes a success," Tanner later noted facetiously.

"After Vanguard," quips Louise Tanner, "the next stop would have been the Yale University Press."

Julian Muller, who was editor-in-chief at Vanguard at that time, remembers, "I had just joined Vanguard two months before I first got a look at the manuscript for *Auntie Mame*. Over a business luncheon with my friend, Elizabeth Otis, the literary agent, we discussed what I was looking for in the way of new projects. I said I wanted to see something funny for a change."

Otis had what she considered seven or eight hilarious chapters – which were really episodic sketches, or unrelated short stories – except they were about one particular character, written by her client Edward Tanner. She suggested that Muller read the work-in-progress.

"I read it over that weekend," Muller remembers. "It was one of the funniest things I had ever come across. I spoke to Elizabeth the following Monday and asked if I could meet with the author, that perhaps we could work something out."

Muller did meet with Tanner and his agent two days later at Otis' apartment in New York. Within an hour, the three of them had sketched out a full-length book using the short stories as a base. But it wasn't ever really a "novel" in the accepted sense of that word.

"There was nothing to cement the various short pieces together," says Muller, "until I decided we should use something like the 'unforgettable character' from *The Readers Digest*, as something that would be kind of a bonding for each chapter, but totally unlike the sweet, serene people they usually had in the *Digest*. Pat [Tanner] just grabbed that idea and ran with it beautifully."

Auntie Mame might have been overlooked as just another of thousands of books that came out that year if it hadn't been for a clever promotional campaign. George Hecht, manager of Doubleday

Bookshops, read the book and liked it so much that he got in touch with James Murphy, sales manager at Vanguard. Hecht suggested that an advertisement be placed promising that Doubleday Bookshops would give two books in return for anyone who read *Auntie Mame* and didn't like it. In addition, Murphy added some advertising gimmicks of his own including matchbooks whose covers asked, "Have you read *Auntie Mame?*"

The successful publication of *Auntie Mame* in 1955 irrevocably altered Tanner's life. With a best-selling book to his credit he retired from *Foreign Affairs* in 1956 and was hired to dramatize his material for Broadway producers Robert Fryer and Lawrence Carr. However, the undertaking proved futile, which surprised everyone since his character dialogue was considered quite brilliant by fans and critics alike.

Over the next 14 years, Tanner continued to write witty, sophisticated stories ("I always start writing with a clean piece of paper and a dirty mind," he said), though none, including *Around the World With Auntie Mame*, a best-selling sequel, ever quite matched the success of the original *Auntie Mame*.

In 1964, when Harcourt/Brace published *The Joyous Season* by Patrick Dennis (which he later acknowledged as his favorite novel), the sales were negligible. The book didn't even make the best-seller lists, and he came to the conclusion that his kind of writing had gone out of style. He felt that he was no longer in demand, and went into semi-retirement.

Coincidentally, Lawrence & Lee were signed to write the screenplay for *The Joyous Season*, which 20th Century Fox had purchased from the galleys. The screenwriters had a romp turning what they considered Pat's funniest book into film-fare. But Fox dropped the project when (unlike *Auntie Mame*) the book never made the best-seller lists.

"I just can't think of new situations any more," Tanner lamented.

221

"I wish I had one of those plot wheels that mixes characters and situations. You know, you just spin it and you get a dethroned queen in a lumber camp."

At this point, the life of Edward Everett Tanner began to take an unusual, almost fiction-like turn. He moved away from his family in New York, and sequestered himself in Mexico for a time, before becoming a partner in an art gallery in Houston, Texas. Several more books followed: *Tony* (1966), *How Firm a Foundation* (1968) and *Paradise* (1971), and in 1972 he penned his last volume, *3-D*.

After the meager sales of *3-D*, Tanner completely changed his life-style. He moved to West Palm Beach, Florida, and became a personal valet – a servant – to the very wealthy.

"Patrick Dennis is dead," he later exclaimed in a letter home. "I killed him with a razor when I hit the Palm Beach airport. The beard is gone and so is the little that was left on top. Now I look like a very old deep sea turtle. That beard covered a lot of sags and wattles."

In September 1973, he wrote to his son Michael about his new career: "With a smart portfolio of references as to my 28 years of experience (the most flattering of which was signed by Patrick Dennis), I have become butler-valet to Stanton Griffis, ambassador to almost every place, and now more or less retired in Palm Beach. He has to be 85. However, he is thinking of remarrying after 35 years of celibacy. If I don't do something frightful like scald massa with a tureen of soup, I may even last. I've certainly trained enough servants of my own to know about serving from the left and removing from the right."

Anticipating the logical question of why he was taking what appeared to be such a bizarre career move, he wrote to his son, "I can't quite explain it to myself. Perhaps it's some sort of penance for my profligate life, like going into a Trappist monastery. If I ever understand it myself, I will try to explain."

In another letter, Tanner implored his son to keep his position a secret. "I would be grateful if you told no one where I am working or what I am doing. It is not that I am ashamed of being a menial – after all, I chose it as being less boring than the Gallery Victor in Houston. It is simply that the news is too funny to keep. I would end up in someone's column and I'd be out on my ass, as they would be certain that I was working there only to spy on them and make sport of them in a new book."

Two months into his new occupation, Tanner revealed to his son that he was an absolute sensation at his job and had never been happier. Referring to his employer, the author wrote, "He's about the dearest old fart on earth, with the manners of a pig and the morals of a goat (an analogy he had previously used to describe a character in *Auntie Mame*), but at 86, his morals are mostly a faint memory. He was the owner of Brentano's [a chain of book stores] and considering that *Auntie Mame* kept that establishment in the black during both 1955 and '56, I was a little miffed when he asked, 'Who is Patrick Dennis?'" – referring to his letter of recommendation.

When Stanton Griffis died in 1974, Tanner accepted a position with the wealthy Mrs. Clive Runnells in Lake Forest, Illinois, and then on to the most interesting assignment of his new career. "I have a new job and it's absolute heaven," he announced in another letter to Michael. "I am working as major domo for Mr. and Mrs. Ray A. Kroc. He is the founding father and chairman of the board of McDonald's. They are the dearest people on earth – nouveau riche (20 years of super affluence) and frank to admit it.

"If anyone has to be burdened with several million dollars, it ought to be the Krocs. Far from being ashamed of their money, they revel in it. And they're not piggy about it like the Hon.

Stan. They pay me $12,000 a year and want to give me more because I'm 'indispensable.' (How would they know? They're never here. I've never laid eyes on Mrs. Kroc, although we talk at length every day on the Watts line. She calls me 'Sweetie!'). He likes to take his meals in our vast chi-chi interior decorated kitchen and always makes me sit down and have a drink with him. (True, it's not done, but what am I supposed to do? Spit in his eye?) Well, I just couldn't have fallen into a better place or with nicer people."

A man of culture, refinement and great taste, Tanner easily portrayed the role of major domo. His employers never had any idea that their manservant, referred to as "Edwards," was famed novelist Patrick Dennis. Philanthropist Joan Kroc remembers "Edwards" and was surprised many years later to learn that she had actually employed the famous creator of Auntie Mame.

*

By May 1976, Tanner reported to his son that, while he was still working, he had been in generally ill health since the previous November. "I have lost 40 pounds since January, and have been unable to keep down so much as a glass of wine. While I would enjoy having an adolescent figure, emaciation is more than I bargained for. I'm vomiting like a pregnant woman and no one seems to know why."

Finally, exhausted and ill, he returned home to Louise in New York, where she cared for him with the aid of a warm and supporting family, an indefatigable household retainer and a loyal group of friends. Patrick faced death without illusions of any kind and in his final months was an inspiration to all. Though he had a couple of projects tentatively on the publishing fire, he had officially retired from writing. "I've said everything I have to say – twice," he joked to his son.

On November 6, 1976, Edward Everett Tanner III (aka Patrick Dennis, Sarah Brooks, Virginia Rowans, Lancelot Leopard, Desmond LaTouche, et al) died in New York, of pancreatic cancer. He was 56 years old.

"As for the disposal of my remains," he had instructed, "it's my chance to go to medical school. However, if you can't find some nice institution to take my body and useable organs, just a quick, cheap cremation and the ashes flushed down a toilet will do. In other words, don't waste a lot of time and effort to dispose of me."

"I think more than anything else, he never wanted to be a bore," his son says. "He wrote to entertain and it was fine with him as long as that was working. I don't think he would have written a third *Auntie Mame* book because he didn't want to be tiresome. 'Don't bore people!' That was one of his guiding principles in life."

"Pat was a renaissance man," says Louise. "His varied artistic endeavors and interests were myriad. There were four or five things he could have done if he hadn't been a writer. He could have been an architect or an interior decorator," she said. "When he came to the end of his life there were three books that he had owned – *Post's Etiquette* a crossword dictionary, and he was fond of Thackary and said he read *Vanity Fair* every year."

"He was extremely accomplished and able to turn out highly-polished material faster than anybody I've ever known," says his editor Julian Muller. "Of course his sense of humor was extraordinary, but he also had a serious side to him. He was well-rounded."

"He was also ahead of his time when it came to equal rights for women," recalls Louise. "When he worked at *Foreign Affairs* magazine, he always said that it was terrible that a man who is stupid can command a much bigger salary than a very intelligent woman. He was always going to bat for the underdog. At one point, there were two very underpaid secretaries, making perhaps $2,000 a year. He pleaded his case to their boss, then took the man out to the subway and retraced the women's daily trip. 'This is what these two ladies have to go through everyday for their small earnings,' he said. After that they both got a raise," Louise remembers.

"Every recollection I have of Pat is with a pleasant expression on his face," notes playwright Robert E. Lee. "He had a sly quality. His wit was very subtle."

Most fascinating about his book *Auntie Mame* was the way Edward Everett Tanner hit some sort of vein that nobody else had ever tapped, that absolutely everybody seems to have a crazy aunt. "I would say that there are very few writers who have actually contributed a household name into our language," says Louise. "People still say, 'Oh, she's an Auntie Mame' and you know immediately what they mean."

Cast List – *Auntie Mame* on Broadway

AUNTIE MAME, produced by Robert Fryer and Lawrence Carr at the Broadhurst Theatre, New York City, opened October 31, 1956, with the following cast, in order of appearance. The production closed June 28, 1958, after 639 performances.

Norah Muldoon	BEULAH GARRICK
Patrick Dennis, as a young man	JAN HANDZLIK
Ito	YUKI SHIMODA
Vera Charles	POLLY ROWLES
Osbert	CRIS ALEXANDER
Ralph Devine	GRANT SULLIVAN
Bishop Eleftharosees	WILLIAM MARTEL
M. Lindsay Woolsey	JOHN O'HARE
Auntie Mame	ROSALIND RUSSELL
Mr. Waldo, a paper hanger	GEOFFREY BRYANT
Mr. Babcock	ROBERT ALLEN
Al Linden, the stage manager	WALLY MOHR
Theatre Manager	WILLIAM MARTEL
Maid	KIP McARDLE
Butler	PAUL LILLY
Leading Man	JAMES FIELD
Lord Dudley	WALTER RIEMER
Customer	KIP McARDLE
Customer's Son	BARRY TOWSEN
Mr. Loomis	CRIS ALEXANDER
Beauregard Jackson Pickett Burnside	ROBERT SMITH
Cousin Jeff	WILLIAM MARTEL
Cousin Fan	NAN McFARLAND
Cousin Moultrie	FRANK ROBERTS

Sally Cato Macdougal...................................MARIAN WINTERS
Emory Macdougal..BARRY BLAKE
Mother Burnside...ETHEL CODY
Fred, a groom...PAUL LILLY
Sam, another groom...JAMES FIELD
Huntsman...CRIS ALEXANDER
Dr. Shurr, a vet..GEOFFREY BRYANT
Patrick Dennis, a young man.........................ROBERT HIGGINS
Agnes Gooch...PEGGY CASS
Brian O'Bannion...JAMES MONKS
Gloria Upson..JOYCE LEAR
Doris Upson...DOROTHY BLACKBURN
Claude Upson..WALTER KLAVUN
Pegeen Ryan..PATRICIA JENKINS
Michael Dennis..JAN HANDZLIK
And a great many friends of Auntie Mame

Cast List – Warner Bros. *Auntie Mame*

Auntie Mame.. ROSALIND RUSSELL
Vera Charles..CORAL BROWNE
Patrick Dennis (as a child)...................................JAN HANDZLIK
Norah Muldoon...CONNIE GILCHRIST
Lindsay Woolsey.. PATRICK KNOWLES
Mr. Babcock...FRED CLARKE
Agness Gooch ....PEGGY CASS
Brian O'Bannion..ROBIN HUGHES
Gloria Upson...JOANNA BARNES
Patrick Dennis (as a young man)........................ROGER SMITH
Beauregard...FORREST TUCKER
Claude Upson ....WILLARD WATERMAN
Doris Upson...LEE PATRICK
Sally Cato..BROOK BYRON
Mrs. Burnside...CAROL VEAZIE
Ito..YUKI SHIMODA

Cast List – *Mame* on Broadway

Mame opened at the Winter Garden Theatre on May 24, 1966, with the following cast, in order of appearance. The production closed January 3, 1970, after 1,508 performances.

Patrick Dennis, age 10................................FRANKIE MICHAELS
Agnes Gooch...JANE CONNELL
Vera Charles...BEATRICE ARTHUR
Mame Dennis...ANGELA LANSBURY
Ralph Devine..RON YOUNG
Bishop...JACK DAVISON
M. Lindsay Woolsey...GEORGE COE
Ito...SAB SHIMONO
Doorman.. ART MATTHEWS
Elevator Boy...STAN PAGE
Messenger...BILL STANTON
Dwight Babcock.....................................WILLARD WATERMAN
Art Model...JO TRACT
Dance Teacher..JOHANNA DOUGLAS
Leading Man..JACK DAVISON
Stage Manager.......................................ART MATTHEWS
Madame Branislowski...............................CHARLOTTE JONES
Gregor ....JOHN TALIAFERRO
Beauregard Jackson Picket Burnside.......CHARLES BRASWELL
Cousin Fan...RUTH RAMSEY
Uncle Jeff...CLIFFORD FEARL
Sally Cato...MARGARET HALL
Mother Burnside....................................CHARLOTTE JONES
Junior Babcock...RANDY KIRBY
Patrick Dennis, age 19-29................................JERRY LANNING

Gloria Upson...DIANA WALKER
Mrs. Upson..JOHANNA DOUGLAS
Mr. Upson..JOHN C. BECHER
Pegeen Ryan...DIANE COUPE
Peter Dennis..MICHAEL MAITLAND

Cast List – Warner Bros. *Mame*

Mame...LUCILLE BALL
Vera.. BEATRICE ARTHUR
Older Patrick..BRUCE DAVISON
Sally Cato...JOYCE VAN PATTEN
Mr. Upson...DON PORTER
Mrs. Upson...AUDREY CHRISTIE
Agnes Gooch..JANE CONNELL
Young Patrick...KIRBY FURLONG
Mr. Babcock..JOHN McGIVER
Gloria Upson..DORIA COOK
Pegeen..BOBBI JORDAN
Ito..GEORGE CHIANG
Beauregard...ROBERT PRESTON

Books by Patrick Dennis

Oh, What a Wonderful Wedding, Crowell, 1953

House Party, Crowell, 1954

Auntie Mame, Vanguard, 1955

Guestward Ho!, Vanguard, 1956

The Loving Couple, Crowell, 1956

The Pink Hotel, Putnam, 1957

Around the World With Auntie Mame, Harcourt, Brace, 1958

Love and Mrs. Sargent, Farrar, Straus, Cudahy, 1961

Little Me, Dutton, 1961

Genius, Harcourt, Brace & World, 1962

First Lady, Morrow, 1964

The Joyous Season, Harcourt, Brace & World, 1964

Tony, Dutton, 1966

How Firm a Foundation, Morrow, 1968

Paradise, Harcourt, Brace, Jovanovich, 1971

3-D, Coward, McCann, Geoghegan, 1972

The Plays of Lawrence & Lee

1948 – *Look, Ma, I'm Dancin'!*

1955 – *Inherit The Wind*

1956 – *Shangri-La*

1956 – *Auntie Mame*

1959 – *The Gang's All Here*

1959 – *Only In America*

1961 – *Checkmate* (formerly entitled *A Call On Kuprin*)

1965 – *Diamond Orchid*

1966 – *Live Spelled Backwards*

1966 – *Mame*

1967 – *Sparks Fly Upward*

1969 – *Dear World*

1970 – *The Crocodile Smile*

1971 – *The Incomparable Max*

1971 – *The Night Thoreau Spent In Jail*

1972 – *Jabberwock*

1973 – *Ten Days That Shook The World* (Lee)

1975 – *Sounding Brass* (Lee)

1977 – *First Monday In October*

1990 – *Whisper In The Mind*

The Musicals of Jerry Herman

1954 – *I Feel Wonderful* (off-Broadway)

1958 – *Nightcap* (off-Broadway)

1960 – *Parade* (off-Broadway)

1961 – *Milk And Honey*

1961 – *Madame Aphrodite* (off-Broadway)

1964 – *Hello, Dolly!*

1966 – *Mame*

1969 – *Dear World*

1974 – *Mack And Mabel*

1979 – *The Grand Tour*

1983 – *La Cage aux Folles*

1985 – *Jerry's Girls*